MANIFEST WITH THE MOON
ASTRO-MOON DIARY 2026

from the I Choose Love Series

Manifest with the Moon Astro-Moon Diary 2026
From the I Choose Love Series

South Africa Standard Time & Central Africa Time edition

Manifest with the Moon Astro-Moon Diary 2026
The Art of Manifestation Astro-Moon Diary & Journal
First Published 2019 A-Z of Emotional Health Ltd.
©2019 Jenny Florence/Burgess The A-Z of Emotional Health Ltd.
Published by the A-Z of Emotional Health Ltd.
Cover Design © Jenny Florence The A-Z of Emotional Health Ltd
with licensed images and fonts from Creative Market and istock

ISBN 978-1-0685284-8-4

All rights reserved. No part of this book may be reproduced by any mechanical, photographic, or electronic process, or in the form of a phonographic recording; nor may it be stored in a retrieval system, transmitted, or otherwise be copied for public use – other than for "fair use" as brief quotations embodied in articles and reviews without prior written permission of the publisher.

The intent of the author is only to offer information of a general nature to assist in an individual's search for emotional and spiritual wellness. In the event that you use any of the information in this

MANIFEST WITH THE MOON
ASTRO-MOON DIARY 2026

This Diary Belongs to

_____

Contents

The Art of Manifestation	1
The Phases of Manifestation	2
The Phases of the Moon	3
How to Use this Diary	4
January	6
February	24
March	40
April	56
May	72
June	90
July	106
August	124
September	140
October	156
November	174
December	190
The Moon in the Zodiac Signs	210
The Void of Course Moon	212
Solar and Lunar Eclipses	213
The Planets in Retrograde	216
The Art of Manifestation Oracle Cards	222
About the Author	223

MANIFEST WITH THE MOON
ASTRO-MOON DIARY 2026

For extra Moon Information, Readings & Webinars, Books, Cards, and Courses, follow Jenny on social media or visit her websites

- https://www.youtube.com/@MoonMagicWeeklyTarot
- https://www.youtube.com/@MoonMagicMonthlyTarot
- https://www.instagram.com/moonmagicjennyflorence/
- https://moonmagicmastertarot.com/
- https://www.azemotionalhealth.com/

The Art of Manifestation

In my career as an Accredited UK registered Counsellor spanning more than 30 years, I have had the privilege to walk alongside literally hundreds of people, who despite facing major stuff in their personal lives, through deep diving into their own psychology and emotions, have overcome their difficulties and moved their lives forward, and indeed are now thriving… and this has given me a passion to explore any tools that can help us to transform and manifest, and this is what started my own magical journey of learning to manifest with the Moon.

Manifestation isn't just about imagining and dreaming about the life you want… you will also need to take actions so that your dreams can find form… and whilst some things can arrive very quickly, other things will take time, spiraling through many phases of the manifestation process.

I have noticed that manifestation follows a natural cyclical pattern and when I started to seriously follow the phases of the Moon, I realized that the influence of the incoming Lunar flow of energy perfectly mirrored the different stages of manifestation.

As I explored the Moon phases further and started to notice and record how this was affecting me personally, I found that the influence of the zodiac sign that the Moon was passing through also had a noticeable effect on the way that I was thinking and feeling.

Learning how the Lunar energy affected me personally changed my take on manifestation completely and opened up a whole new way of living… more effectively… more fruitfully… more productively… more peacefully… and more spiritually… in fact, all aspects of my life, both personally and professionally, have changed for the better!

So, let's take a look at the phases of manifestation, and then the phases of the Moon, the parallel is amazing!

The Phases of Manifestation

1. You decide you want something, and you give yourself permission to believe in this possibility… and to dream.
2. Now you will need to take some sort of steps towards this, whether big or small… and commit to moving forwards and doing what it takes to get started.
3. Review and ongoing evaluation are then needed… manifestation happens one step at a time… you may need to tweak your direction… or work out how to overcome any obstacles to your progress… clarity of ongoing direction comes through objective evaluation.
4. Excitement and energy builds… you commit, you invest, and you persevere.
5. As progress unfolds, whether in your external actions or deep within your own psyche, the universe will show you what is needed to keep your energy flowing. So, you'll need to observe and listen… what is working and what isn't? And then actively use this information to validate your purpose and direction… and if needed, let go of whatever isn't working… cleanse and release… so you can commit fully to the journey ahead.
6. Holding a clarity of mind, you are now wiser and stronger, you continue with steady progress.
7. In steady momentum, trusting that the universe knows your fullest potential and holds a higher vision that is greater than you could possibly imagine, remember to pause, and evaluate along the way… there is always opportunity to make adjustments and tweak the details.
8. As your pathway emerges and your dreams begin to take form, remember to slow down, and enjoy the journey. Life is for living and being too fixed on the future can actually slow your manifestations down! Be balanced… slow and steady wins the race… and periods of stillness will often open avenues of new potential.

And a new cycle begins… you listen to your desires, and you give yourself permission to believe and to dream. Some of your manifestations will be ongoing, with a new phase building on the foundation of the last… whilst others will be completely new, fresh ideas born of experiences that forge new desires.

The Phases of the Moon

1. The New Moon is traditionally associated with the setting of wishes and intentions and the energy naturally invites you to dream of possibilities.
2. In the phase of the Crescent Moon the seeds that emerged at the New Moon call to be heard. In manifestation, we are both doers and deciders… it's time to respond and be proactive in taking steps, however small or large.
3. The First Quarter Moon is a time of evaluation, so look carefully at the scope of your ideas and use this energy to focus on the actions that are most important at this moment in time… review and formulate your goals for the rest of the month.
4. In the Gibbous Moon phase energy is building, passions are high, and dreams call to be made real. Enjoy the excitement of anticipation but remain present and grounded. Commit, invest, and persevere.
5. The brightness and power of the highly charged Full Moon energy brings a space of authenticity where all is revealed and illuminated, so notice and listen, particularly to any situations that seem to demand your attention. The energy of this phase of the Moon brings a wonderful opportunity to notice, to listen, to reflect, and then to release and let go, clearing the way to move forwards.
6. The Disseminating Moon phase invites authentic empowerment. Be steady in your actions and in your doings, stand in your power and be your true self with joy, gratitude, and humility, and affirm your dedication to your pathway.
7. The energy of the Last Quarter Moon invites you to walk your talk, so stand back and review, and make sure your plans, actions, and decisions are congruent with all that you wish to see in the world, and if need be, tweak and adjust.
8. The Balsamic Moon asks you to trust. Hold your vision, and yet simultaneously let go of any attachment to specific outcomes. This is a time of preparation and nurture. Validate, acknowledge, and cherish all your achievements and as this Lunar cycle comes to its completion prepare the ground for your own deliverance and the beginning of a new cycle of opportunity.

And a new cycle begins… you listen to your desires, and you give yourself permission to believe and to dream. Some of your manifestations will be ongoing, with a new phase building on the foundation of the last… whilst others will be completely new, fresh ideas born of experiences that forge new desires.

How to Use this Diary

Knowing about the ebb and flow and flavor of the incoming Lunar lens ahead of time is a major tool of empowerment.

When I started to follow the Moon on a daily basis, I realized very quickly that the incoming Lunar energy was touching and influencing my emotions and my thoughts, and even my physical wellbeing as well, and especially my energy levels… all of which then affected my overall attitude, mood, and state of mind.

I could see tangible variations in how relaxed I was feeling… or how stressed I was… whether I felt confident, resilient, and durable… or ultra-sensitive and far more vulnerable… whether I felt motivated or stuck… focused or all over the place… all of this and more… and so, I started to make notes about the way that the incoming Lunar energy was affecting me personally and these notes became a reference point for me…

The Moon always follows a consistent pattern, sometimes increasing and accelerating, and sometimes diminishing and easing, with peaks of greater intensity along the way. This energy is then in turn flavored by the personality and characteristics of the Zodiac sign that the Moon is passing through, creating a kind of 'Lunar Lens' of the day. This is also influenced further as the Moon passes by and connects with the other major planetary alignments that are happening… and the phases of the Moon also happen to align perfectly with the stages of manifestation…

This diary was born as a result of my observations and my experiences. It is designed to give you exactly the information that you need to build a personal record of how the Lunar energy affects you personally, so you can then align your daily living and ongoing manifestations with the incoming influence of the Moon. In my personal experience, the more awareness you have of the incoming flow of Lunar energy, the more empowered you are. It's like having a personal GPS that lets you know ahead of time about any speed limits… whether the flow of traffic is fast and unrestricted… or busy but steady… or if there are roadworks and diversions ahead… you may need to slow down… or even take a different route!

To give you the heads up of what's coming, at the start of each month there's an overview of the incoming influences… plus a detailed energy write up for every Moon phase… and additional guidance from Oracle Cards and Runes to help you navigate with awareness.

The week to view pages then tell you the phase and zodiac sign of the Moon every day… plus extra astrological information… and there is space for you to make notes and record your own experiences.

And at the back you'll find a ton of extra information, including…

- A description of the influence of each Zodiac sign on the energy of the Moon as she passes through each sign.
- VOC – Information about the Void of Course Moon. (VOC – you'll see this in the diary pages)
- The influence and meaning of Solar and Lunar eclipses.
- Information about the planets in retrograde, with listings of the dates that these events occur throughout the year.

Further reading…

If you are really serious about manifesting with the Moon, you may also wish to use the Manifest with the Moon Workbook & Journal which takes you to a whole other layer of Moon magic!

This book focuses on the wisdom of the Thirteen Moons of the Celtic Tree Lore and Tribal Traditions, and I share my own personal experiences of the deeper psychological layers of Soul growth that unfolded in my life as I listened and learned from the Moon… for me this deeper layer of learning was absolutely life changing!

Desires, Goals and Intentions for January 2026

Welcome to January 2026

January 2026. The Re-structure Begins...

2026 begins with dissolution and restructure which are at the top of the planetary agenda! And so the first half of the month could present some testing moments... but with a higher purpose... the energetics invite you to become the witness self and be an observer of your own experiences... so you can then consciously use the shifts and increasing flow of energy that unfold as the month progresses.

Supported and enhanced by our beautiful Moon, the astro-dynamics in the latter part of January offer huge opportunities for rebirth, restructure, and expansion with the potential to see real results that can emerge, take shape, and gather momentum...

So even though there may be a few bumps in the road along the way, January is a month that encourages you to dream big and think big whilst simultaneously keeping sight of the bigger picture and your place and part in the emergence of a new humanity and the collective whole.

As always our Cards and Runes give a clear indication of how best to harness and align with the overall energy flow of energy for the month... Dagaz, the Rune of Breakthrough, aligns with the card of Forgiveness of Ourselves, suggesting opportunities for genuine breakthrough moments, creating change and transformation from the inside out, and removing blockages that may have previously held you back from stepping into the very best version of you... whilst our second card of Choices and Decisions aligning with Nauthiz, the Rune of Constraint urges patience... acknowledging that restructure, change, and evolutionary transformation takes time... and even when solutions are apparent it can take time to work out how best to implement these changes in real terms.

Overall... the astro-dynamics of the month offer an amazing opportunity to observe and then take action, supported by a flow of expanding energy that whilst not entirely without challenge, brings opportunities and openings that create a space of genuine growth and possibility in real terms.

Cards and Runes January 2026

Cards and Runes January 2026

Choices and Decisions
6

The choices that we make today are defining the shape of our tomorrow and so it is hardly surprising that we sometimes worry about making the right decisions. Do not shroud your mind in the fog of uncertainty. Just as you have choices today, you also have choices tomorrow, and the day after...
Be assured, you can always change course again.

7 - Nauthiz - The Rune of Constraint

Obstacles. Restrictions. Frustration and irritation.
Use this time wisely. Cross the T's and dot the I's.
When Fishman can't go to see they meant their nets.
Observe your situation with humour.
Setbacks are a form of guidance, view your situation through this perspective. You may need to reconsider your plans.
Rectification comes before progress.

Moon Phases January 2026

 The Waxing Gibbous Moon – from 28 December to 2 January passing through Aries, Taurus, Gemini, and into Cancer

The overall astro-dynamics of this Moon phase hold a flavour of deep and profound healing… and although, from time to time, there are some spikes of stronger energy… and in the build up to the Full Moon the energetics intensify further, throughout this period, the Lunar influence is backing the overall energetic of profound healing 100% … so you can be sure that whatever emerges, it is arriving to be acknowledged and healed. At the entry point to a New Year we naturally focus on what we hope to achieve and to manifest over the coming months and then set New Year resolutions to support these wishes and dreams, so this is a great time to establish goals for the coming year that promote healing, balance, and the well-being of all.

 The Full Moon – 3 January – 13°01' Cancer

The planetary alignments of this Moon bring positivity and forward motion… the energy is vibrant, creative, balanced, and absolutely loaded with possibility… with an undertone that supports new and possibly unexpected opportunities… so use the energy of this dynamic and potentially auspicious day to your advantage…
Science tells us that your mind is an active participant in shaping the world you are creating, and the energetics today are primed for success and expansion so be conscious of your thoughts and harness the energy through the power of focused thought, whilst also opening yourself to potential windows of opportunity that could arrive suddenly! If you need to resolve imbalances in your life… or release emotional baggage with ease… or receive guidance to expand and move forwards… the energy will support you! So get focused!

Full Moon Global Timings:
Los Angeles, USA   Sat, 3 Jan 2026 at 02:02 PST
New York, USA   Sat, 3 Jan 2026 at 05:02 EST
Reykjavik, Iceland   Sat, 3 Jan 2026 at 10:02 GMT
London, UK   Sat, 3 Jan 2026 at 10:02 GMT
Paris, France   Sat, 3 Jan 2026 at 11:02 CET
Cape Town, SA   Sat, 3 Jan 2026 at 12:02 SAST
Delhi, India   Sat, 3 Jan 2026 at 15:32 IST
Perth, Australia   Sat, 3 Jan 2026 at 18:02 AWST
Tokyo, Japan   Sat, 3 Jan 2026 at 19:02 JST
Sydney, Australia   Sat, 3 Jan 2026 at 21:02 AEDT
Auckland, NZ   Sat, 3 Jan 2026 at 23:02 NZDT
GMT/UTC   Sat, 3 Jan 2026 at 10:02 GMT

The Disseminating or Waning Gibbous Moon – from 4 January to 9 January passing through Cancer, Leo, Virgo, and into Libra

This essence of this Moon phase continues the theme of expansion that was so powerful at the Full Moon… and the Lunar influence adds a steadying influence that suggests the potential for genuine real progress, particularly in any areas of emotional turbulence, self-doubt, or low self-esteem… so use this time well as healing is promoted.
For the 24 hours before the Last Quarter Moon the energy suddenly and significantly heats up… so be aware of this… if anything unexpected shows up you are far more likely to find the answers from within than from external sources… so use this Moon phase to initially be productive but also be prepared to slow down and get still if circumstances call you to do so.

 The Last Quarter Moon – 10 January – 20°24' Libra

A last Quarter Moon invites growth through the inner work of reflection and personal review, supporting self-empowerment through self-awareness that leads to self-mastery. Now this Moon is intense to put it mildly! And yet it also holds much potential with an underlying energetic that supports personal growth and expansion arising from holding a balanced perspective…
It is quite possible that some tetchiness and frustrations could surface at this time and that buttons could be pressed… The key to using this energy is to align with the reflective essence of this Moon phase, supported by balanced Libra, and make a conscious personal choice to notice your own reactions and responses, especially any internal feelings and thinking patterns, before then choosing how you respond in any situation!

 The Balsamic Moon or Waning Crescent Moon – from 11 January to 17 January passing through Scorpio, Sagittarius, and into Capricorn

The intensity of the Last Quarter Moon remains constant throughout this period. Despite the Moons diminishing and softening influence, there is an underlying flow of expansion, escalation, and movement suggesting great potential to expand through taking a positive, proactive, approach in all of your dealings… however in any areas of your world that are running less than smoothly it could feel as though circumstances are moving too fast or feel a bit out of control. If this is the case then put down an anchor and lean into your daily meditation practise… the planetary influences support out-of-the-box higher minded solutions… and sometimes it is tension that creates traction… and restructure through awareness really is the name of the game at this time!

The New Moon – 18 January – 28°43' Capricorn

Every New Moon heralds a new start and a new beginning and after the rather hectic underlying energy of the Balsamic Moon phase our first New Moon of 2026 really is bringing in some lighter energy… however, this doesn't necessarily mean quiet and peaceful!
Restructure is ongoing at this time and Uranus, the great awakener, is about to station direct after a long retrograde period, which can herald the potential for sudden shifts and changes… but given the overriding positivity of the energy today, if anything shifts suddenly it is highly likely to be happening in a beneficial and auspicious way, aiding the process of fast paced evolutionary change! So be sure to set your New Moon wishes and intentions especially in areas of your manifestations where you are hoping for fast results.

New Moon Global Timings:
Los Angeles, USA	Sun, 18 Jan 2026 at 11:51 PST
New York, USA	Sun, 18 Jan 2026 at 14:51 EST
Reykjavik, Iceland	Sun, 18 Jan 2026 at 19:51 GMT
London, UK	Sun, 18 Jan 2026 at 19:51 GMT
Paris, France	Sun, 18 Jan 2026 at 20:51 CET
Cape Town, SA	Sun, 18 Jan 2026 at 21:51 SAST
Delhi, India	Mon, 19 Jan 2026 at 01:21 IST
Perth, Australia	Mon, 19 Jan 2026 at 03:51 AWST
Tokyo, Japan	Mon, 19 Jan 2026 at 04:51 JST
Sydney, Australia	Mon, 19 Jan 2026 at 06:51 AEDT
Auckland, NZ	Mon, 19 Jan 2026 at 08:51 NZDT
GMT/UTC	Sun, 18 Jan 2026 at 19:51 GMT

The Waxing Crescent Moon – from 19 January to 25 January passing through Aquarius, Pisces, Aries, and into Taurus

The overall flow of energy during this Moon phase is absolutely delightful… this is a time of profound shift, and the energetics of this Moon time are creating a steady flow of forward motion that supports transitions of higher purpose… so seize the moment…

To use the energy at its best, rather than racing ahead, imagine yourself embarking on a journey where progression is ensured, however you are advised to take a gentle and responsive approach.

Centre yourself in absolute trust… be open to synchronicities… take ownership of your own agency, your own empowerment, and your own personal choices… and follow through with real actions. The energy intensifies just before the First Quarter Moon, so if anything isn't flowing smoothly trust that this is bringing valuable information and arriving with purpose.

The First Quarter Moon – 26 January – 06°14' Taurus

The energy and higher purpose of a First Quarter Moon is to bring clarity and clear direction so we can successfully move forwards… and often heralds external events and circumstances arriving to highlight any obstacles that need to be overcome to clear the pathway ahead. The dynamics today are pushing for rebirth… and Neptune moves into Aries… and this major event will enhance the energy of the day, bringing the perfect opportunity for you to be shown exactly what you need to see to ensure ongoing successful progression in all areas of your ongoing manifestations. The energy today is strong so be conscious of this! If at all possible, schedule time today to be still and hold the position of the witness self… and observe rather than pushing forwards… as this will pay dividends to assist in finding focus and clarity.

 The Waxing Gibbous Moon – from 27 January to 1 February passing through Taurus, Gemini, and Cancer

Following an intense First Quarter Moon, the dynamics open up and with renewed clarity and loaded with positivity the energy flows yet again with the Moon adding weight and gathering momentum to your manifestations! In fact… the energy is so strong that it is worthy of being mindful not to push so fast and furiously that ambitions and desire override compassion, and awareness of others, and the bigger picture! So use this energy well… think big and be prepared to take action and commit to your dreams and your pathway ahead… but be mindful at the same time… the energy could really help to turn dreams into reality… but if you are swept along by potential success and ego gets in the way, the energy will also soon highlight any areas where actions are not in alignment with higher purpose and intent.

December 2025 / January 2026

---

29 Monday
Aries • VOC (9h 46m) • Taurus

Waxing Gibbous Moon

---

30 Tuesday
Taurus

Waxing Gibbous Moon

---

31 Wednesday
Taurus • VOC (49m) • Gemini

Waxing Gibbous Moon
New Year's Eve

---

1 Thursday
Gemini

Waxing Gibbous Moon
2026 begins with Jupiter, Uranus, and Chiron in Retrograde
New Year's Day

---

2 Friday
Gemini • VOC (46m) • Cancer

Waxing Gibbous Moon Phase ends
Chiron Retrograde Ends

January 2026

Journalling and Notes

---

3   Saturday
Cancer

Full Moon 13°01' Cancer

---

4   Sunday
Cancer • VOC (46m) • Leo

Waning Gibbous Moon Phase starts

January 2026

---

5 Monday
Leo

Waning Gibbous Moon

---

6 Tuesday
Leo • VOC (3h 53m) • Virgo

Waning Gibbous Moon
Venus Star Point 16° 22' Capricorn

---

7 Wednesday
Virgo

Waning Gibbous Moon

---

8 Thursday
Virgo

Waning Gibbous Moon

---

9 Friday
Virgo • VOC (44m) • Libra

Waning Gibbous Moon Phase ends

January 2026

Journalling and Notes

---

10 Saturday

Libra • VOC (17h 3m)

Last Quarter Moon 20°24' Libra

---

11 Sunday

VOC • Scorpio

Waning Crescent Moon Phase starts

January 2026

12 Monday
Scorpio

Waning Crescent Moon

13 Tuesday
Scorpio

Waning Crescent Moon

14 Wednesday
Scorpio • VOC (36m) • Sagittarius

Waning Crescent Moon

15 Thursday
Sagittarius

Waning Crescent Moon

16 Friday
Sagittarius • VOC (29m) • Capricorn

Waning Crescent Moon

January 2026

Journalling and Notes

17 Saturday
Capricorn

Waning Crescent Moon Phase ends

18 Sunday
Capricorn • VOC (22m)

New Moon 28°43' Capricorn

January 2026

19 Monday

VOC • Aquarius

Waxing Crescent Moon Phase starts
Martin Luther King Jr. Day - USA

---

20 Tuesday

Aquarius

Waxing Crescent Moon
Sun Enters Aquarius

---

21 Wednesday

Aquarius • VOC (4h 34m) • Pisces

Waxing Crescent Moon

---

22 Thursday

Pisces

Waxing Crescent Moon

---

23 Friday

Pisces • VOC (10m) • Aries

Waxing Crescent Moon

January 2026

Journalling and Notes

---

24 Saturday
Aries • VOC (20h 30m)

Waxing Crescent Moon

---

25 Sunday
VOC • Taurus

Waxing Crescent Moon Phase ends

January 2026

26 Monday
Taurus

First Quarter Moon 06°14' Taurus
Neptune Enters Aries
Australia Day Public Holiday

27 Tuesday
Taurus • VOC (2h 58m) • Gemini

Waxing Gibbous Moon Phase starts

28 Wednesday
Gemini

Waxing Gibbous Moon

29 Thursday
Gemini • VOC (2h 36m)

Waxing Gibbous Moon

30 Friday
VOC • Cancer

Waxing Gibbous Moon

January / February 2026

Journalling and Notes

31 Saturday
Cancer • VOC (2h 18m)

Waxing Gibbous Moon

1 Sunday
VOC • Leo

Waxing Gibbous Moon Phase ends
St Brigid's Day , Festivals of Imbolc Northern Hemisphere - Lammas Southern Hemisphere

Desires, Goals and Intentions for February 2026

Welcome to February 2026

February 2026. Expect the Unexpected!

As a general rule, within this diary I prefer to speak in terms of energy rather than use astrological language, which I hope makes the information more widely accessible… however… this month heralds some major astrological events… and so…

On the 13th Saturn crosses the world axis point moving into Aries where he will remain until 2028… and then on 20th he joins Neptune in an exact conjunction… and suffice it to say, this is BIG energy! The last time Saturn and Neptune joined in an exact conjunction the Berlin Wall came down! And Saturn and Neptune have not joined forces on this pivotal point of 0 degrees Aries for thousands of years! Now Saturn and Neptune danced closely together back in 2025, so we may find ourselves returning to certain issues that were around at that time, and now… with the potential for these circumstances to move forwards and become established in real terms. The overall astro-dynamics also suggest a flavour of unpredictability… perhaps some sudden and unexpected twists and turns in events and circumstances… so overall this looks to be an interesting month for us all… both personally and globally.

Our Cards and Runes for this month are fascinating… The card of You are Safe Now feels like a statement of reassurance from the Universe at a time when upheaval and the uncertainty of accelerated change are in full motion… and suggesting that despite uncertainty… all will be well… and this card aligns with Nauthiz the Rune of Constraint which asks us to view frustrations and restrictions as guidance bringing an invitation to cross the T's and dot the I's so as to improve the potential outcome…

Followed by our second card of Problems, which again reinforces the Spiritual perspective that identifying a problem is the perfect route to creating a potential solution… this card then aligns with Sowelu, The Rune of Wholeness… this is Rune of great power that symbolises victory and that there is only one way to move forwards… the pathway to wholeness and your relationship with the whole!

Wow… what a month!

Cards and Runes February 2026

Cards and Runes February 2026

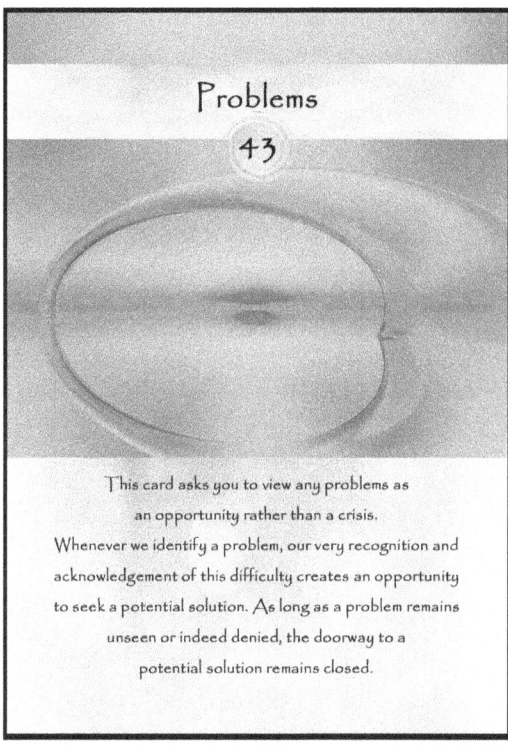

Problems 43

This card asks you to view any problems as an opportunity rather than a crisis. Whenever we identify a problem, our very recognition and acknowledgement of this difficulty creates an opportunity to seek a potential solution. As long as a problem remains unseen or indeed denied, the doorway to a potential solution remains closed.

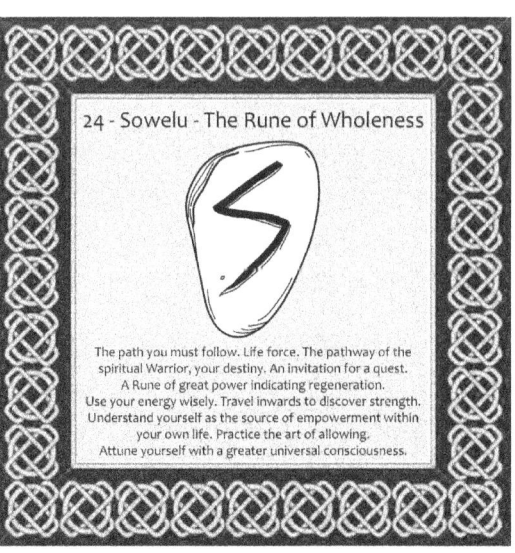

24 - Sowelu - The Rune of Wholeness

The path you must follow. Life force. The pathway of the spiritual Warrior, your destiny. An invitation for a quest. A Rune of great power indicating regeneration. Use your energy wisely. Travel inwards to discover strength. Understand yourself as the source of empowerment within your own life. Practice the art of allowing. Attune yourself with a greater universal consciousness.

Moon Phases February 2026

 The Waxing Gibbous Moon – from 27 January to 1 February passing through Taurus, Gemini, and Cancer

Following an intense First Quarter Moon, the dynamics open up and with renewed clarity and loaded with positivity the energy flows yet again with the Moon adding weight and gathering momentum to your manifestations! In fact… the energy is so strong that it is worthy of being mindful not to push so fast and furiously that ambitions and desire override compassion, and awareness of others, and the bigger picture! So use this energy well… think big and be prepared to take action and commit to your dreams and your pathway ahead… but be mindful at the same time… the energy could really help to turn dreams into reality… but if you are swept along by potential success and ego gets in the way, the energy will also soon highlight any areas where actions are not in alignment with higher purpose and intent.

 The Full Moon – 2 February – 13°03' Leo

In the build up to this dynamic Moon, the planetary alignments create an auspicious Kite formation with a cluster of planets at the head in higher minded Aquarius and the Moon at the base, in big, bold Leo… and today is also the Earth festival of Imbolc in the Northern Hemisphere and Lammas in the Southern Hemisphere, both festivals of fertility… and we are approaching Eclipse season… and Saturn will soon be crossing the Earth's axis and moving into Aries again… and this may create opportunities for to get something going and get it off the ground… or at the very least illuminate how you got to where you are, and what you will need to do to move forwards… and give you the courage and confidence to take action! So be brave and courageous… and be prepared to take a significant leap forward if the opportunity presents itself!

Full Moon Global Timings:
Los Angeles, USA   Sun, 1 Feb 2026 at 14:08 PST
New York, USA   Sun, 1 Feb 2026 at 17:08 EST
Reykjavik, Iceland Sun, 1 Feb 2026 at 22:08 GMT
London, UK   Sun, 1 Feb 2026 at 22:08 GMT
Paris, France   Sun, 1 Feb 2026 at 23:08 CET
Cape Town, SA   Mon, 2 Feb 2026 at 00:08 SAST
Delhi, India   Mon, 2 Feb 2026 at 03:38 IST
Perth, Australia   Mon, 2 Feb 2026 at 06:08 AWST
Tokyo, Japan   Mon, 2 Feb 2026 at 07:08 JST
Sydney, Australia   Mon, 2 Feb 2026 at 09:08 AEDT
Auckland, NZ   Mon, 2 Feb 2026 at 11:08 NZDT
GMT/UTC   Sun, 1 Feb 2026 at 22:08 GMT

The Disseminating or Waning Gibbous Moon – from 3 February to 8 February passing through Leo, Virgo, Libra, and into Scorpio

The overall astrodynamics of this Moon phase feels a bit up and down... although there is a lovely undercurrent of positivity, there are also some distinctly spiky surges of intense energy as well, supporting an underlying energetic of unpredictability... and although they are relatively fleeting, this could suggest an overall flavour of fast-paced happenings... and with a distinctly Karmic flavour as well. If you are actively restructuring and reorganising, these pockets of dynamic intensity may serve you well... but if you are feel as though life is happening too fast and you to want to slow down or even stop... this period could feel a little bit testing... so try to remain grounded and use the more gentle pockets of energy to take a breather, rather than pushing ahead regardless.

 The Last Quarter Moon – 9 February – 20°46' Scorpio

The energy of today's Moon honours the truth and is primed with the potential to reveal undercurrents and underlying issues... and they may arrive unexpectedly... so today could potentially bring some sudden or even unexpected revelations! Now this isn't necessarily negative... you may find that events and circumstances arrive to consolidate and confirm your inner feelings and perspectives... however, you could equally find that conversations, events, or circumstances reveal areas of discord or discomfort. The key to this energy is to observe... a Last Quarter Moon promotes agency through internal examination and discovery and our beautiful Moon is also moving into a very favourable alignment that promotes restructure through heightened intuition and spiritual awareness... so listen up and use the energy well!

 The Balsamic Moon or Waning Crescent Moon – from 10 February to 16 February passing through Scorpio, Sagittarius, Capricorn, and Aquarius

This Moon time heralds a major astrological shift and the flow of energy begins with a fairly concentrated karmic flavour, suggesting the potential for some intense communications and negotiations... however, whether events are happening globally, or in the immediacy of your personal world, our beautiful Moon will be softening these pockets of intensity... and whether passionately positive... or more challenging... the dynamics also favour higher minded solutions and out of the box thinking, and with the Lunar influence also slowing the energy down... whatever is taking place, with awareness of this, you can harness your passion for the outcome you desire, with an equal desire to find a process that creates this outcome in a fair and balanced and harmonious way.

The New Moon Annular Solar Eclipse – 17 February – 28°49' Aquarius (See Eclipse Moons p.213)

Welcome to Eclipse Season… a time of Karmic potential! An Eclipse Moon is said to open a portal that shows the timeline between the past… the present… and the future… rather like your dreams, which can do the same.
A New Moon is a time of new beginnings when we set wishes and intentions and sow seeds of all that we wish to manifest. This New Moon is dynamic and connects with a very strong energy of uncertainty and unpredictability suggesting the potential for unexpected happenings, and in quite practical earthy areas of our lives… however, there is also a planetary collaboration that favours flowing communications that expand and bring benefit. So, if anything shows up today that is unexpected, trust that rather like a dream, it is a form of communication arriving as guidance… and may well be steering you in a particular direction to support your wishes and intentions.

New Moon Global Timings:
Los Angeles, USA	Tue, 17 Feb 2026 at 04:13 PST
New York, USA	Tue, 17 Feb 2026 at 07:13 EST
Reykjavik, Iceland	Tue, 17 Feb 2026 at 12:13 GMT
London, UK	Tue, 17 Feb 2026 at 12:13 GMT
Paris, France	Tue, 17 Feb 2026 at 13:13 CET
Cape Town, SA	Tue, 17 Feb 2026 at 14:13 SAST
Delhi, India	Tue, 17 Feb 2026 at 17:43 IST
Perth, Australia	Tue, 17 Feb 2026 at 20:13 AWST
Tokyo, Japan	Tue, 17 Feb 2026 at 21:13 JST
Sydney, Australia	Tue, 17 Feb 2026 at 23:13 AEDT
Auckland, NZ	Wed, 18 Feb 2026 at 01:13 NZDT
GMT/UTC	Tue, 17 Feb 2026 at 12:13 GMT

 The Waxing Crescent Moon – from 18 February to 23 February passing through Pisces, Aries, and Taurus

The Waxing Crescent Moon phase is all about getting started… getting going… and getting things off the ground… and the Lunar influence gradually and steadily grows and builds in strength. This Moon Time begins with a flavour of Karmic justice, and so with Saturn and Neptune inching closer and closer to their exact meeting point it will be interesting to see what unfolds, both personally and on the global stage. The overall flow of Lunar energy is then relatively steady, so even though big transformations and restructure are a central focus, use this time to be conscious of your own personal responses and reactions, as this will pay dividends during the more intense periods of astro-dynamics. In the last couple of days of this Moon phase the Moons growing energy will add to some stronger, more heated dynamics that suggest the potential for some impulsive, or erratic, or unpredictable events, circumstances, and responses… so remain grounded, centred, and observe before responding.

The First Quarter Moon – 24 February – 05°54' Gemini

This Moon invites you to look ahead, and the energy today suggests opportunities to understand situations and perspectives from all sides… and to evaluate with an emphasis on finding positive and optimistic outcomes and solutions that honour justice, fairness, equality, and balance. Yea!!!
There is also an underlying Karmic presence that brings a sense of destiny, suggesting that the opportunity to review or the subjects and areas of our lives that we are reviewing may not be a surprise… it is as if the Universe has been waiting for the best moment to call us to account, and whether personally or globally, give us a window of opportunity to think ahead to the future that we wish to create and then plan accordingly!

 The Waxing Gibbous Moon – from 25 February to 2 March passing through Gemini, Cancer, Leo, and into Virgo

During this phase the overall energy can be divided into two halves. The first half suggests significant intensity with the potential for emotions to run high… and yet, despite the intensity, there is still a strong underlying flavour of possibility present, and although these possibilities could arise through tension or frustrations, the higher purpose is to support movement forwards, even if this involves interruptions and diversions or situations that stretch you out of your comfort zone… so try to be flexible! In the second half, the energy levels out, and although still expanding, it is steadier, so in areas of your life that are naturally growing, the first part of this period will help you define any problems that can then in the second half, be resolved and transformed, ideally through reflection. But, if you experience tension or frustrations and cannot see how best to proceed, then if at all possible press the pause button and wait for the Full Moon to bring illumination and guidance before moving ahead.

February 2026

2 Monday

Leo

Full Moon 13°03' Leo

---

3 Tuesday

Leo • VOC (4h 27m) • Virgo

Waning Gibbous Moon Phase starts

---

4 Wednesday

Virgo

Waning Gibbous Moon
Uranus Retrograde Ends

---

5 Thursday

Virgo • VOC (1h 45m) • Libra

Waning Gibbous Moon

---

6 Friday

Libra

Waning Gibbous Moon
Waitangi Day NZ

February 2026

Journalling and Notes

---

7 **Saturday**
Libra • VOC (7h 14m) • Scorpio

Waning Gibbous Moon

---

8 **Sunday**
Scorpio

Waning Gibbous Moon Phase ends

February 2026

9 Monday

Scorpio

Last Quarter Moon 20°46' Scorpio

10 Tuesday

Scorpio • VOC (22m) • Sagittarius

Waning Crescent Moon Phase starts

11 Wednesday

Sagittarius

Waning Crescent Moon

12 Thursday

Sagittarius • VOC (17m) • Capricorn

Waning Crescent Moon

13 Friday

Capricorn

Waning Crescent Moon

February 2026

Journalling and Notes

14 Saturday

Capricorn

Waning Crescent Moon
Saturn Enters Aries
Valentine's Day

15 Sunday

Capricorn • VOC (4h 46m) • Aquarius

Waning Crescent Moon

February 2026

16 Monday
Aquarius

Waning Crescent Moon Phase ends
Presidents Day USA

17 Tuesday
Aquarius • VOC (2h 9m) • Pisces

The New Moon Annular Solar Eclipse 28°49' Aquarius

18 Wednesday
Pisces

Waxing Crescent Moon Phase starts
Sun Enters Pisces

19 Thursday
Pisces • VOC (4h 17m) • Aries

Waxing Crescent Moon

20 Friday
Aries

Waxing Crescent Moon
Saturn Conjunct Neptune

February 2026

Journalling and Notes

---

21 Saturday

Aries • VOC (12h 20m)

Waxing Crescent Moon

---

22 Sunday

VOC • Taurus

Waxing Crescent Moon

February 2026

23 Monday
Taurus

Waxing Crescent Moon Phase ends

24 Tuesday
Taurus • VOC (4h 1m) • Gemini

First Quarter Moon 05°54' Gemini

25 Wednesday
Gemini

Waxing Gibbous Moon Phase starts

26 Thursday
Gemini • VOC (6h 12m) • Cancer

Waxing Gibbous Moon
Mercury Retrograde Begins

27 Friday
Cancer

Waxing Gibbous Moon

February / March 2026

Journalling and Notes

28 Saturday
Cancer • VOC (3h 56m) • Leo

Waxing Gibbous Moon

1 Sunday
Leo

Waxing Gibbous Moon

Desires, Goals and Intentions for March 2026

Welcome to March 2026

March 2026. Fate… Destiny… and Karmic Re-birth… You are the Source of Change in your World!

March is a big month with renewal at the top of the agenda… and whether this is in the context of your personal world or on the global stage, the overall astro-energy suggests events and circumstances may emerge that need to be addressed and call for rebirth and restructure in real terms… and there is a very distinct flavour of fate and destiny throughout!

It is possible that circumstances that have remained unresolved could well resurface during this month… or perhaps similar situations may arise that resonate or mirror previous events… however, whatever lands in your world, the purpose of this is to find successful conclusions and completions and start to build new systems and structures that embody the high vibrational qualities of fairness, equality, and integrity, and through open and honest communications, create pathways forward that lead to a long term sustainable future, not only for ourselves and our personal foreseeable future circumstances, but also for our beautiful planet and for future generations yet to come.

Our first card of Uncertainty sits with Thurisaz the Rune of Gateway. I find the imagery in this card fascinating, because this is a Rune that metaphorically calls you to climb to the top of a mountain… get still… and meditate… observe all of the events that have led you to be where you are in this moment in time… and then with full awareness of the way that the past has influenced the present… and with gratitude for your learning… to step through the gateway and proceed. And the card of Uncertainty honours your right to take your time when you are making important decisions and choices, especially at a time of uncertainty and escalated transformation.

Our second card of Walk Your Talk literally invites you to 'Be the Change You Wish to See in the World' and aligning with Inguz the Rune of Fertility, which promises favourable results… this combination is a direct invitation for you to step up and become your own personal hero or heroine and create positive change through being the very best version of yourself.

Cards and Runes March 2026

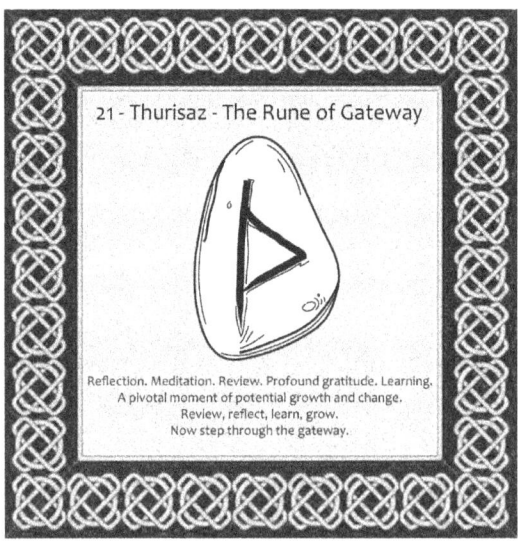

Cards and Runes March 2026

Moon Phases March 2026

The Waxing Gibbous Moon – from 25 February to 2 March passing through Gemini, Cancer, Leo, and into Virgo

During this phase the overall energy can be divided into two halves. The first half suggests significant intensity with the potential for emotions to run high... and yet, despite the intensity, there is still a strong underlying flavour of possibility present, and although these possibilities could arise through tension or frustrations, the higher purpose is to support movement forwards, even if this involves interruptions and diversions or situations that stretch you out of your comfort zone... so try to be flexible! In the second half, the energy levels out, and although still expanding, it is steadier, so in areas of your life that are naturally growing, the first part of this period will help you define any problems that can then in the second half, be resolved and transformed, ideally through reflection. But, if you experience tension or frustrations and cannot see how best to proceed, then if at all possible press the pause button and wait for the Full Moon to bring illumination and guidance before moving ahead.

The Full Moon Total Lunar Eclipse – 3 March – 12°53' Virgo (See Eclipse Moons p.213)

The energetics of this Full Moon Total Eclipse invite you to think into the future through conscious awareness of the past... and the planetary collaborations today form a melting pot of possibility! This Moon brings the potential to observe and become aware of yourself... and others... and situations or circumstances... and then from a deep, compassionate, perhaps even driven place from within, work out how best to proceed and plan ahead. If there was ever a Moon that favoured a day of complete stillness and meditation then this is it! So even if you have a packed or demanding day, try to make some time somewhere to get still and notice, observe, and listen...

Full Moon Global Timings:
Los Angeles, USA   Tue, 3 Mar 2026 at 03:37 PST
New York, USA   Tue, 3 Mar 2026 at 06:37 EST
Reykjavik, Iceland Tue, 3 Mar 2026 at 11:37 GMT
London, UK   Tue, 3 Mar 2026 at 11:37 GMT
Paris, France   Tue, 3 Mar 2026 at 12:37 CET
Cape Town, SA   Tue, 3 Mar 2026 at 13:37 SAST
Delhi, India   Tue, 3 Mar 2026 at 17:07 IST
Perth, Australia   Tue, 3 Mar 2026 at 19:37 AWST
Tokyo, Japan   Tue, 3 Mar 2026 at 20:37 JST
Sydney, Australia   Tue, 3 Mar 2026 at 22:37 AEDT
Auckland, NZ   Wed, 4 Mar 2026 at 00:37 NZDT
GMT/UTC   Tue, 3 Mar 2026 at 11:37 GMT

The Disseminating or Waning Gibbous Moon – from 4 March to 10 March passing through Virgo, Libra, Scorpio, and Sagittarius

The essence and energy of the Full Moon lingers for a couple of days... so as we enter this Moon phase, if all possible, continue to hold space for stillness, observation, listening, and noticing...
The energy then begins to flow, and even though Mercury is in Retrograde the overall dynamics of this Moon time have a gentle and yet meaningful flavour... so go with the flow and let the Universe be your guide, and if any diversions or interruptions occur then go with it... this is a pocket of time when letting the tide steer you, rather than trying to hold a fixed course may prove to be the most productive and beneficial approach. Right at the end of this period the Moon leans into some particularly creative energy so be conscious of this window of opportunity.

 The Last Quarter Moon – 11 March – 20°49' Sagittarius

Given the fairly laid back, go with the flow, feel of the previous Moon phase, this Moon time brings a slightly more intense energy... however, this energy is actually in perfect attunement with the very essence of everything that a Last Quarter Moon is traditionally associated with... inviting you to evaluate from the inside out and through internal reflection and evaluation, align your thoughts, words, and actions with your true values and step up and walk your talk...
So in areas of your world that are going well this could feel like a pocket of validation or consolidation, however, if you are navigating big stuff... after all our world is in a process of profound accelerated growth... then make some time for internal reflection and personal journalling and try to assess and evaluate from the perspective of your own personal choice and empowerment.

 The Balsamic Moon or Waning Crescent Moon – from 12 March to 18 March passing through Capricorn, Aquarius, and Pisces

The energy of this Moon phase suggests some powerful dynamics of drive, impetus, and activity... though not always without friction... and a strong flavour of fate and destiny thrown into the mix! So don't be surprised if events and circumstances bring things to light that require or even demand your attention... and if you do find yourself having to respond, then try to align with the Lunar influence which is bringing a more 'slow and steady wins the race' kind of flavour, inviting a mindful, spiritually centred approach to find solutions that create new systems and perspectives that support long term sustainable possibilities.

The New Moon – 19 March – 28°27' Pisces

In the turbulence of massive global and personal transformation, this New Moon brings a breath of fresh air and a magical point of power!

Sitting right on the cusp of Pisces and Aries and aligning with the four day window of shift and turn that occurs at the equinoxes… this is the spring equinox in the Northern hemisphere, and the autumn equinox in the Southern hemisphere… the energy today is not just primed to get going… it is turbocharged!

This is a day when your manifestations can get a serious boost and be launched to the next level… and this includes the removal of any blocks or challenges, or aspects of life that no longer serve you. So, align your dreams, wishes, and desires, with higher purpose and the greatest good for all… send them out into the universe see what comes back!

New Moon Global Timings:
Los Angeles, USA	Wed, 18 Mar 2026 at 18:23 PDT
New York, USA	Wed, 18 Mar 2026 at 21:23 EDT
Reykjavik, Iceland	Thu, 19 Mar 2026 at 01:23 GMT
London, UK	Thu, 19 Mar 2026 at 01:23 GMT
Paris, France	Thu, 19 Mar 2026 at 02:23 CET
Cape Town, SA	Thu, 19 Mar 2026 at 03:23 SAST
Delhi, India	Thu, 19 Mar 2026 at 06:53 IST
Perth, Australia	Thu, 19 Mar 2026 at 09:23 AWST
Tokyo, Japan	Thu, 19 Mar 2026 at 10:23 JST
Sydney, Australia	Thu, 19 Mar 2026 at 12:23 AEDT
Auckland, NZ	Thu, 19 Mar 2026 at 14:23 NZDT
GMT/UTC	Thu, 19 Mar 2026 at 01:23 GMT

 ### The Waxing Crescent Moon – from 20 March to 24 March passing through Aries, Taurus, and Gemini

This Moon phase begins on the exact day of the equinox symbolising a major turning point… and the Mercury retrograde period, which is often associated with delays and disruptions, comes to an end. This combination of energy is then followed by some very flowing planetary collaborations… which are in turn propelled by the Moon's gathering energy, inviting and supporting progression. So whether you are working on something that is brand new… or something that is ongoing… and whether this is internal or external, this is an incredibly favourable Moon time to initiate a fresh start or a new phase of development… and the dynamics are favourable throughout… so what are you waiting for… get going!

The First Quarter Moon – 25 March – 05°08' Cancer

This Moon connects directly with the phenomenal energy of restructure that is currently influencing humanity at large, and it is not only humanity that is responding to the planetary energies... nature and Earth herself are calling for change.
Traditionally a First Quarter Moon brings external circumstances and events to help you to identify / resolve / climb up / climb over... any hurdles or obstacles to your progress... and whether this day brings personal insight or more global perspectives, this Moon time is also favourably underpinned with an energetic that suggests windows of opportunity that promote and activate rebirth and transformation, particularly through higher minded solutions that align with the bigger picture... so if at all possible, take time today to observe and notice... significant insights may well come to light that support powerful and effective change!

 The Waxing Gibbous Moon – from 26 March to 1 April passing through Cancer, Leo, Virgo, and into Libra

The energy of this period is BIG! During any Waxing Gibbous Moon phase, the Lunar influence is strengthening and naturally heralds expansion... however in this particular Moon time, the underpinning astro-dynamics are calling for sound solid evaluation, leading to re-structure and re-birth and in real terms! This is underpinned by a terrific flow of energy that looks to gather momentum, rather like a river, growing in strength as it moves towards the sea... and this momentum also has a distinctly karmic feel to it, as if destiny and fate may have a hand in the events and circumstances that unfold at this time. There are also some strong spikes of energy that push for change and transformation and healing through open, honest communications, so don't be surprised if events unfold that call you to action... and if they do, navigate with care and integrity!

March 2026

2 Monday

Leo • VOC (7m) • Virgo

Waxing Gibbous Moon Phase ends

3 Tuesday

Virgo

Full Moon Total Lunar Eclipse 12°53' Virgo

4 Wednesday

Virgo • VOC (4h 4m) • Libra

Waning Gibbous Moon Phase starts

5 Thursday

Libra

Waning Gibbous Moon

6 Friday

Libra • VOC (28h 40m)

Waning Gibbous Moon

March 2026

Journalling and Notes

7 **Saturday**
VOC • Scorpio

Waning Gibbous Moon

8 **Sunday**
Scorpio

Waning Gibbous Moon
USA & Canada Clocks Change

March 2026

9 Monday

Scorpio • VOC (4h 10m) • Sagittarius

Waning Gibbous Moon

10 Tuesday

Sagittarius

Waning Gibbous Moon Phase ends

11 Wednesday

Sagittarius • VOC (18h 29m)

Last Quarter Moon 20°49' Sagittarius
Jupiter Retrograde Ends

12 Thursday

VOC • Capricorn

Waning Crescent Moon Phase starts

13 Friday

Capricorn

Waning Crescent Moon

March 2026

Journalling and Notes

14 Saturday
Capricorn • VOC (3h 42m) • Aquarius

Waning Crescent Moon

15 Sunday
Aquarius

Waning Crescent Moon
UK Mother's Day

March 2026

16 Monday
Aquarius • VOC (3h 20m)

Waning Crescent Moon

17 Tuesday
VOC • Pisces

Waning Crescent Moon
Saint Patrick's Day

18 Wednesday
Pisces

Waning Crescent Moon Phase ends

19 Thursday
Pisces • VOC (2h 40m) • Aries

The New Moon 28°27' Pisces

20 Friday
Aries • VOC (21h 12m)

Waxing Crescent Moon Phase starts
Sun Enters Aries, Mercury Retrograde Ends
Spring Equinox Northern Hemisphere - Autumn Equinox Southern Hemisphere

March 2026

Journalling and Notes

21 Saturday
VOC • Taurus

Waxing Crescent Moon

22 Sunday
Taurus

Waxing Crescent Moon

March 2026

23 Monday
Taurus • VOC (2h 40m) • Gemini

Waxing Crescent Moon

24 Tuesday
Gemini

Waxing Crescent Moon Phase ends

25 Wednesday
Gemini • VOC (11h 57m) • Cancer

First Quarter Moon 05°08' Cancer

26 Thursday
Cancer

Waxing Gibbous Moon Phase starts

27 Friday
Cancer • VOC (2h 30m) • Leo

Waxing Gibbous Moon

March 2026

Journalling and Notes

28 Saturday

Leo

Waxing Gibbous Moon

29 Sunday

Leo • VOC (2h 7m) • Virgo

Waxing Gibbous Moon
UK & Central Europe Clocks Change

Desires, Goals and Intentions for April 2026

Welcome to April 2026

April 2026. Bring on the New!

Although April brings some undeniably strong planetary configurations suggesting the possibility that frustrations may occur... there is also an underlying strength of determination present in the overall dynamics that can really assist in navigating change... onwards and upwards and on all levels!

From a spiritual perspective the astro-dynamics are set to open enhanced channels of communication... and there are some very favourable alignments that indicate advancements, innovation, and forward thinking... with opportunities to shift old habits and patterns that no longer serve... including underlying issues that may have previously remained unseen or unresolved being brought to light at a time of favourable potential outcomes... this is definitely not a month to remain stuck or still...

Given these dynamic planetary collaborations our cards and Runes are fascinating! Our first card of Intention highlights the power of your thoughts, and aligned with Laguz, the Rune of Flow... which curiously enough is attuned with the energy of the Moon... this suggests that this is a month when we can begin to genuinely master our capacity to actively manifest... indeed, science may even bring forth evidence that advances and confirms our knowledge of this process...

Our second card of You are Safe Now aligning with Kano, the Rune of Openings seems to imply that in these epic times of monumental change and accelerated growth, we can finally relax into the process of transformation rather than be phased by it... Kano is a powerful Rune that indicates a point of opening, where we move from a period of darkness... perhaps unconsciousness... into light and enhanced awareness...

I am intrigued to see what emerges!

Cards and Runes April 2026

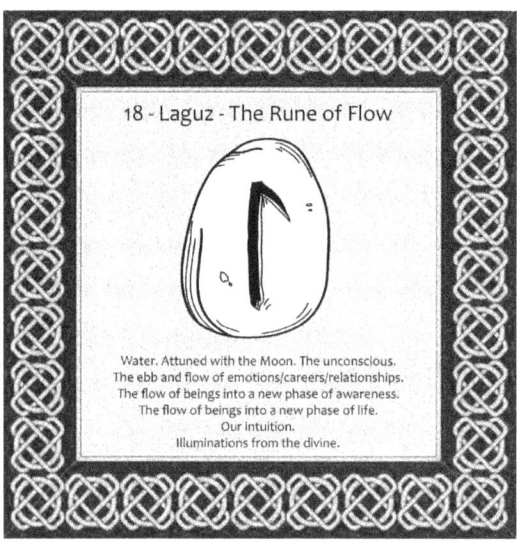

Cards and Runes April 2026

Moon Phases April 2026

 The Waxing Gibbous Moon – from 26 March to 1 April passing through Cancer, Leo, Virgo, and into Libra

The energy of this period is BIG! During any Waxing Gibbous Moon phase, the Lunar influence is strengthening and naturally heralds expansion… however in this particular Moon time, the underpinning astro-dynamics are calling for sound solid evaluation, leading to re-structure and re-birth and in real terms! This is underpinned by a terrific flow of energy that looks to gather momentum, rather like a river, growing in strength as it moves towards the sea… and this momentum also has a distinctly karmic feel to it, as if destiny and fate may have a hand in the events and circumstances that unfold at this time. There are also some strong spikes of energy that push for change and transformation and healing through open, honest communications, so don't be surprised if events unfold that call you to action… and if they do, navigate with care and integrity!

 The Full Moon – 2 April – 12°21' Libra

When I look at the chart of this Moon, the qualities that immediately spring to mind are… truth, honesty, justice, equality, fairness, balance, and integrity… and this Moon invites you to embrace these qualities through self-mastery and personal choice. A Full Moon is traditionally thought to illuminate what we need to see so we can take appropriate action, whether to let go of something that no longer serves… or to step forwards… or both, and the overall flavour of this Moon promotes action… the energy is fiery and yet also flowing, and with an undercurrent that suggests the potential for changeability and rapid events. So if something in your world shows up suddenly or unexpectedly, you can be sure it is arriving with the purpose of aligning you with all of the high vibrational qualities that are embodied in the energy of the day.

Full Moon Global Timings:
Los Angeles, USA	Wed, 1 Apr 2026 at 19:11 PDT
New York, USA	Wed, 1 Apr 2026 at 22:11 EDT
Reykjavik, Iceland	Thu, 2 Apr 2026 at 02:11 GMT
London, UK	Thu, 2 Apr 2026 at 03:11 BST
Paris, France	Thu, 2 Apr 2026 at 04:11 CEST
Cape Town, SA	Thu, 2 Apr 2026 at 04:11 SAST
Delhi, India	Thu, 2 Apr 2026 at 07:41 IST
Perth, Australia	Thu, 2 Apr 2026 at 10:11 AWST
Tokyo, Japan	Thu, 2 Apr 2026 at 11:11 JST
Sydney, Australia	Thu, 2 Apr 2026 at 13:11 AEDT
Auckland, NZ	Thu, 2 Apr 2026 at 15:11 NZDT
GMT/UTC	Thu, 2 Apr 2026 at 02:11 GMT

The Disseminating or Waning Gibbous Moon – from 3 April to 9 April passing through Libra, Scorpio, Sagittarius, and Capricorn

Right at the beginning of this Moon phase the Lunar influence is reasonably steady... so take advantage of this, because the energy then intensifies and with an emphasis on relationships... particularly the emotional undercurrents of your connections and how you feel... so... how do you feel about yourself... about others... and about your relationship to your external circumstances... your home, your working world, and the stuff of your life? We then see an interesting shift in energy that could suggest a desire to break away from restrictions, so it'll be interesting to see how this period pans out. This changeable energy could bring greater excitement and spontaneity into your relationships but if you are in any way uncertain about any connections in your world, then hold fire and wait for the Last Quarter Moon's space of evaluation before moving forwards.

 The Last Quarter Moon – 10 April – 20°20' Capricorn

Given the rather fascinating dynamics of the previous Moon phase, the flavour of this Last Quarter Moon emphasis possibility, bringing a fabulous pocket of time to review and evaluate.
The Lunar influence flows through the ambitious and yet also very practical and pragmatic energy of Capricorn... and with other planetary alignments emphasizing creativity and new beginnings, with awareness of personal choice, your own self-mastery and your own self-empowerment... but also with awareness of others... this is definitely a good day to look ahead and formulate plans for the future. A Last Quarter Moon invites you to walk your talk and to be conscious of the part that you play in creating your personal circumstances... so be sure to align your goals and desires with all that you wish to see in the world.

 The Balsamic Moon or Waning Crescent Moon – from 11 April to 16 April passing through Aquarius, Pisces, and Aries

This Moon time begins with a strong surge of energy that suggests heightened emotions... so if changes were indicated during your Last Quarter Moon review, you may now feel the emotional impact of these possibilities. The Moon then aligns with some dynamic connections that request change and transformation, and even though our beautiful Moon brings a softening energy, the overall undercurrents have a fast pace about them... and so this could be amazing or a little bit too fast and therefore confusing, so be mindful of this. The dynamics also suggest the potential for signs and synchronicities that could bring specific areas of your world into focus... so throughout this period, try to be consciously steady... whilst being simultaneously flexible and open to change.

The New Moon – 17 April – 27°28' – Aries

The essence and overall astrodynamics of today's New Moon are intense and focused... the Moon makes a powerful connection that is calling for healing and there is also a strong push to address any underlying issues that have remained buried or kept beneath the surface, so a heightened emotional vulnerability could well be present today, however the alignments also suggest that channels of spiritual communication will be wide open, bringing the potential for incredible moments of inspiration, imagination, and creativity... so lean into a space of creativity and give your imagination a free reign... but, given the strength of the heightened intensity... also try to remain grounded... and whatever fires you up today and inspires you... apply this to your New Moon wishes and intentions, with conscious awareness that your wishes, dreams, thoughts, words, and deeds are contributing to the emergence of a new humanity.

New Moon Global Timings:
Los Angeles, USA	Fri, 17 Apr 2026 at 04:51 PDT
New York, USA	Fri, 17 Apr 2026 at 07:51 EDT
Reykjavik, Iceland	Fri, 17 Apr 2026 at 11:51 GMT
London, UK	Fri, 17 Apr 2026 at 12:51 BST
Paris, France	Fri, 17 Apr 2026 at 13:51 CEST
Cape Town, SA	Fri, 17 Apr 2026 at 13:51 SAST
Delhi, India	Fri, 17 Apr 2026 at 17:21 IST
Perth, Australia	Fri, 17 Apr 2026 at 19:51 AWST
Tokyo, Japan	Fri, 17 Apr 2026 at 20:51 JST
Sydney, Australia	Fri, 17 Apr 2026 at 21:51 AEST
Auckland, NZ	Fri, 17 Apr 2026 at 23:51 NZST
GMT/UTC	Fri, 17 Apr 2026 at 11:51 GMT

 The Waxing Crescent Moon – from 18 April to 23 April passing through Taurus, Gemini, Cancer, and into Leo

This waxing Crescent Moon phase embodies the flavour of the astro-energy for April, inviting us to embrace advancements and opportunities, and to see things differently and to do things differently, and to shift old habits and patterns and attitudes that no longer serve. And although the overall flow of energy is strong, it is also favourable! When the Moon passes through Cancer, the Lunar influence creates a surge of stronger energetics, suggesting the potential for heightened emotionality... so if you find yourself feeling a bit wobbly, uncertain, or confused then try not to react... the overall flow of positive opportunity alongside the ongoing underlying energetic of determination should help to counterbalance any confusion and help you to stay on track.

The First Quarter Moon – 24 April – 03°56' Leo

This Moon brings a surge of extremely positive energy that suggests excitement and positive advancements. A First Quarter Moon is traditionally associated with events and circumstances that arrive to show us exactly what is needed to move through and beyond any problems…. or indeed to enhance and improve areas of our lives that are already working… and enable them to work even better! Today the overall energetics suggest a surge of positive possibilities that support the breaking out of routines and habits that no longer serve and the finding of new and innovative ways to transform and to grow. This is a day when embracing change could feel joyous and exciting rather than daunting or fearful, so use the energy well and lean into the opportunities to enhance your progress.

 The Waxing Gibbous Moon – from 25 April to 30 April passing through Leo, Virgo, Libra, and into Scorpio

This Moon phase is a mixed bag and potentially a bit of a roller coaster in terms of shifts and changes. Although a flow of underlying positivity is present throughout, the dynamics suggest a potential for unexpected events and circumstances… The higher vibrational energies could bring dynamic advancements and the emergence of new technologies… however, the same dynamics also suggest erratic and impulsive behaviour with rapid or chaotic change and the growing Moon adds weight to this… and there is also a strong karmic feel bringing a flavour of fate and destiny, so this period could be exciting, but also a bit unpredictable… so be conscious of this and lean into the highest vibration of the changes that are occurring!

March / April 2026

30 Monday
Virgo

Waxing Gibbous Moon

31 Tuesday
Virgo

Waxing Gibbous Moon

1 Wednesday
Virgo • VOC (2h 20m) • Libra

Waxing Gibbous Moon Phase ends

2 Thursday
Libra • VOC (27h 17m)

Full Moon 12°21' Libra

3 Friday
VOC • Scorpio

Waning Gibbous Moon Phase starts
Good Friday

April 2026

Journalling and Notes

4 Saturday
Scorpio

Waning Gibbous Moon

5 Sunday
Scorpio • VOC (2h 4m)

Waning Gibbous Moon
Easter Day, Australia & New Zealand Clocks Change

April 2026

6 Monday
VOC • Sagittarius

Waning Gibbous Moon
Easter Monday Bank Holiday - UK

7 Tuesday
Sagittarius

Waning Gibbous Moon

8 Wednesday
Sagittarius • VOC (2h 14m) • Capricorn

Waning Gibbous Moon

9 Thursday
Capricorn

Waning Gibbous Moon Phase ends

10 Friday
Capricorn

Last Quarter Moon 20°20' Capricorn

April 2026

Journalling and Notes

---

11 **Saturday**
Capricorn • VOC (1h 33m) • Aquarius

Waning Crescent Moon Phase starts

---

12 **Sunday**
Aquarius

Waning Crescent Moon

April 2026

13 Monday
Aquarius • VOC (1h 14m) • Pisces

Waning Crescent Moon

14 Tuesday
Pisces

Waning Crescent Moon

15 Wednesday
Pisces • VOC (58m) • Aries

Waning Crescent Moon

16 Thursday
Aries

Waning Crescent Moon Phase ends

17 Friday
Aries • VOC (4h 7m) • Taurus

New Moon 27°28' Aries

April 2026

Journalling and Notes

---

18 Saturday

Taurus

Waxing Crescent Moon Phase starts

---

19 Sunday

Taurus • VOC (34m) • Gemini

Waxing Crescent Moon

April 2026

---

20 Monday

Gemini • VOC (35h 43m)

Waxing Crescent Moon
Sun Enters Taurus

---

21 Tuesday

VOC • Cancer

Waxing Crescent Moon

---

22 Wednesday

Cancer

Waxing Crescent Moon

---

23 Thursday

Cancer • VOC (14m) • Leo

Waxing Crescent Moon Phase ends

---

24 Friday

Leo

First Quarter Moon 03°56' Leo

April 2026

Journalling and Notes

25 Saturday
Leo

Waxing Gibbous Moon Phase starts
Anzac Day - Australia & NZ

26 Sunday
Leo • VOC (1m) • Virgo

Waxing Gibbous Moon

Desires, Goals and Intentions for May 2026

Welcome to May 2026

May 2026. New Solutions… Innovations… And Discoveries!

May brings us the first Super Moon of 2026 and this is sandwiched into two Full Moons, both in this month of May… and when we have two Full Moons in one calendar month the second Moon is known as a Blue Moon. This extra Lunar activity energetically intensifies the influence of the Moon, and the overall astro-dynamics of this month, enhanced by the Lunar activity suggest events that call for humanity at large to step up with forward thinking… underpinned by open, authentic conversations… initiate actions that move towards establishing a future of stability that is based on the higher values of integrity, fairness, equality, balance, and harmony… and the planetary alignments look to push for this!

Sometimes this will flow… but there are also some intense moments when we may revisit elements of the past that have yet to be resolved… so be prepared to step up… but also to do so mindfully and with conscious awareness of how your actions now are impacting on the future yet to come.

Our cards of Restore Balance followed by Open Yourself to Possibility says it all! It is time to re-establish balance… to open ourselves to new innovations and new ways of seeing, thinking, and doing… and to start to grow a future worthy of generations yet to come.

Aligning with Teiwaz the Rune of The Spiritual Warrior and with Jeera the Rune of Harvest… this combination suggests that this is a month when discernment will be called for, with a cutting away of the old to clear the way for the new. Interestingly the Rune of Harvest sometimes indicates a period of a year before a harvest comes to fruition… and whilst this supports the overall message of looking ahead and mindfully sowing seeds for the future that we wish to create… given that the energetics also suggest that we may be called to revisit the past, it is also possible that initiatives that you took a year ago may now come to fruition.

Cards and Runes May 2026

Cards and Runes May 2026

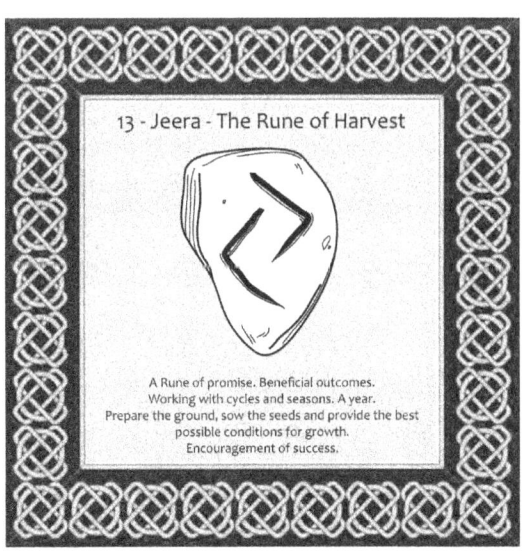

Moon Phases May 2026

 The Full Moon – 1 May – 11°20' Scorpio

This Moon encourages deep introspection and transformation with opportunity to then take action, letting go of anything that is no longer relevant to your growth… so if anything in your world seems to have run its course, the dynamics today suggest an opportunity to evaluate, and then from a deeply personal perspective, initiate changes. Unexpected communications, conversations, and out of the box solutions that focus on healing and reconciliation are highlighted so in areas of discord there could be valuable progress, and anything that is already running smoothly, solutions that support and enhance your progress could show up… and unexpectedly.

Full Moon Global Timings:
Los Angeles, USA   Fri, 1 May 2026 at 10:22 PDT
New York, USA   Fri, 1 May 2026 at 13:22 EDT
Reykjavik, Iceland   Fri, 1 May 2026 at 17:22 GMT
London, UK   Fri, 1 May 2026 at 18:22 BST
Paris, France   Fri, 1 May 2026 at 19:22 CEST
Cape Town, SA   Fri, 1 May 2026 at 19:22 SAST
Delhi, India   Fri, 1 May 2026 at 22:52 IST
Perth, Australia   Sat, 2 May 2026 at 01:22 AWST
Tokyo, Japan   Sat, 2 May 2026 at 02:22 JST
Sydney, Australia   Sat, 2 May 2026 at 03:22 AEST
Auckland, NZ   Sat, 2 May 2026 at 05:22 NZST
GMT/UTC   Fri, 1 May 2026 at 17:22 GMT

 The Disseminating or Waning Gibbous Moon – from 2 May to 8 May passing through Scorpio, Sagittarius, Capricorn, and into Aquarius

The dynamics of this phase suggest some erratic peaks and troughs and being alert to this will help you to harness the very best of this energy… so be open and aware of potential possibilities, and be prepared to take the initiative and dare to do things differently. At times of transition when the energy is pushing full steam ahead there is often some sort of resistance… or simply just some bumps in the road… so be conscious of this and be prepared to expand even if things feel a bit tumultuous… and be innovative in your approach. If you feel motivated and driven then this period will be helpful, but if the pace of change feels a bit demanding then slow down, but remain open to positive change.

The Last Quarter Moon – 9 May – 19°14' Aquarius

The previous Moon time suggested innovative potentials, albeit in a rather up and down way with some very strong pushy waves of energy coming in. A Last Quarter Moon naturally invites you to align with the higher vibrational energy of everything that you wish to see in the world… and the energetics today really support the consolidation of all that was developing during the previous Moon phase. So if at all possible, schedule some time today to pause and reflect, either to consolidate your plans… or, if you are feeling out of balance to create space to regroup and realign.

 The Balsamic Moon or Waning Crescent Moon – from 10 May to 15 May passing through Aquarius, Pisces, Aries, and into Taurus

Overall, the dynamics of this phase suggest a rather sparkly flavour of potential expectation and possibility… and yet the energy flow is also steady. It is almost as though we can tune into a much bigger galactic picture, with recognition that both individually and collectively it is time for humanity to get our act together, with the Lunar influence both holding us to account… and yet also bringing support… so keep going… and go gently with yourself and others… and if the Universe delivers you a few gentle nudges along the way, it is simply to keep you moving in the right direction!

 The Super New Moon – 16 May – 25°57' Taurus

A Super Moon means that the Moon is closer to the Earth, adding additional power to her magnetic strength… and this is turn adds strength to any New Moon wishes and intentions that you choose to set today. Science tells us that our thoughts influence our personal and immediate circumstances, and this Moon invites you to recognise that your impact stretches way beyond this! We are all related and everything is connected… and this Moon asks you to integrate this concept into your life in real terms. Our world needs balance and healing… so get still and think ahead and with genuine intent, commit to your part in creating stability now… and a sustainable future for generations yet to come.

New Moon Global Timings:
Los Angeles, USA   Sat, 16 May 2026 at 13:00 PDT
New York, USA   Sat, 16 May 2026 at 16:00 EDT
Reykjavik, Iceland   Sat, 16 May 2026 at 20:00 GMT
London, UK   Sat, 16 May 2026 at 21:00 BST
Paris, France   Sat, 16 May 2026 at 22:00 CEST
Cape Town, SA   Sat, 16 May 2026 at 22:00 SAST

Delhi, India   Sun, 17 May 2026 at 01:30 IST
Perth, Australia   Sun, 17 May 2026 at 04:00 AWST
Tokyo, Japan   Sun, 17 May 2026 at 05:00 JST
Sydney, Australia   Sun, 17 May 2026 at 06:00 AEST
Auckland, NZ   Sun, 17 May 2026 at 08:00 NZST
GMT/UTC   Sat, 16 May 2026 at 20:00 GMT

The Waxing Crescent Moon – from 17 May to 22 May – passing through Taurus, Gemini, Cancer, and Leo

The Waxing Crescent Moon phase is all about getting started and getting going… and sometimes this can be gentle and steady… but sometimes fast and happening… and this period looks to be fast, with the potential for breakthroughs, and with revelations and awakenings throughout to launch you into new realms of possibility. The first half of this phase suggests opportunities flowing with ease… however, in the second half the dynamics suggest possible friction… so be prepared to be adaptable throughout, and if the pace of your world speeds up, then try to consciously jump on board with this.

The First Quarter Moon – 23 May – 02°20' Virgo

This Moon engages directly with a massive karmic influence that promises to bring heightened awareness of how the past has led to our current circumstances, highlighting what needs to be overcome so you can proceed, and this Moon in practical Virgo may well bring circumstances that require attention to detail… and some of these events could arrive unexpectedly! But awareness of history and attention to detail is not about being critical… indeed if you have a raging inner critic that gets in your way, you may even be called to address this! Liberation from the old is the flavour of the day today, with the potential to bring issues into awareness so as to activate and create new ways of doing things that forge a new direction and a new future.

The Waxing Gibbous Moon – from 24 May to 30 May passing through Virgo, Libra, Scorpio, and into Sagittarius

Throughout this period very strong dynamics are at play with an undercurrent that suggests the returning to issues that have remained unresolved… particularly in areas of injustice or inequality or inappropriate use of power. Despite the strength of the more challenging astrological aspects there is also an undertone of equally strong positivity… and fascinatingly, whenever the more discordant collaborations intensify… so too does the undertone of positivity…

highlighting the potential to seek resolution. These energies could surface in a personal way or more globally, but either way, whatever is happening you can choose how you respond and which of these energies you decide to align with.

 ### The Full Moon – A Blue Moon – 31 May – 09°55' Sagittarius

Today is a Blue Moon, which means it is the second Full Moon in a calendar month. On the 1st the Scorpio Moon asked you to identify and release anything that no longer served you and throughout the month the dynamics have brought ample opportunity to evaluate what is working and what isn't! A Full Moon is always an ideal time to create ceremonies of release and to reset your goals and perspectives and the dynamics today feel remarkably freeing… so take advantage of this and use this Moon to realign your personal energy with positivity and optimism.

Full Moon Global Timings:
Los Angeles, USA   Sun, 31 May 2026 at 01:44 PDT
New York, USA   Sun, 31 May 2026 at 04:44 EDT
Reykjavik, Iceland   Sun, 31 May 2026 at 08:44 GMT
London, UK   Sun, 31 May 2026 at 09:44 BST
Paris, France   Sun, 31 May 2026 at 10:44 CEST
Cape Town, SA   Sun, 31 May 2026 at 10:44 SAST
Delhi, India   Sun, 31 May 2026 at 14:14 IST
Perth, Australia   Sun, 31 May 2026 at 16:44 AWST
Tokyo, Japan   Sun, 31 May 2026 at 17:44 JST
Sydney, Australia   Sun, 31 May 2026 at 18:44 AEST
Auckland, NZ   Sun, 31 May 2026 at 20:44 NZST
GMT/UTC   Sun, 31 May 2026 at 08:44 GMT

April / May 2026

27 Monday
Virgo • VOC (21h 52m)

Waxing Gibbous Moon

28 Tuesday
VOC • Libra

Waxing Gibbous Moon

29 Wednesday
Libra

Waxing Gibbous Moon

30 Thursday
Libra • VOC (10h 11m) • Scorpio

Waxing Gibbous Moon Phase ends

1 Friday
Scorpio

Full Moon 11°20' Scorpio
Festivals of Beltane Northern Hemisphere – Samhain Southern Hemisphere

May 2026

Journalling and Notes

2 **Saturday**
Scorpio • VOC (21h 47m)

Waning Gibbous Moon Phase starts

3 **Sunday**
VOC • Sagittarius

Waning Gibbous Moon

May 2026

---

4 Monday

Sagittarius • VOC (21h 33m)

Waning Gibbous Moon
Early May Bank Holiday - UK

---

5 Tuesday

VOC • Capricorn

Waning Gibbous Moon

---

6 Wednesday

Capricorn

Waning Gibbous Moon
Pluto Retrograde Begins

---

7 Thursday

Capricorn • VOC (17h 10m)

Waning Gibbous Moon

---

8 Friday

VOC • Aquarius

Waning Gibbous Moon Phase ends

May 2026

Journalling and Notes

9 Saturday
Aquarius

Last Quarter Moon 19°14' Aquarius

10 Sunday
Aquarius • VOC (12h 32m) • Pisces

Waning Crescent Moon Phase starts
Mother's Day - USA, Canada, Australia, & New Zealand

May 2026

11 Monday

Pisces

Waning Crescent Moon

12 Tuesday

Pisces • VOC (14h 1m)

Waning Crescent Moon

13 Wednesday

VOC • Aries

Waning Crescent Moon

14 Thursday

Aries • VOC (4h 59m)

Waning Crescent Moon

15 Friday

VOC • Taurus

Waning Crescent Moon Phase ends

May 2026

Journalling and Notes

16 Saturday

Taurus

Super New Moon 25°57' Taurus

17 Sunday

Taurus • VOC (1h 22m) • Gemini • VOC (30h 11m)

Waxing Crescent Moon Phase starts

May 2026

---
18 Monday

VOC

Waxing Crescent Moon

---
19 Tuesday

VOC • Cancer

Waxing Crescent Moon

---
20 Wednesday

Cancer • VOC (13h 22m)

Waxing Crescent Moon

---
21 Thursday

VOC • Leo

Waxing Crescent Moon
Sun Enters Gemini

---
22 Friday

Leo • VOC (32h 52m)

Waxing Crescent Moon Phase ends

May 2026

Journalling and Notes

---

23 Saturday
VOC • Virgo

First Quarter Moon 02°20' Virgo

---

24 Sunday
Virgo

Waxing Gibbous Moon Phase starts

May 2026

25 Monday
Virgo • VOC (13h 41m) • Libra

Waxing Gibbous Moon
Spring Bank Holiday - UK, Memorial Day - USA

26 Tuesday
Libra

Waxing Gibbous Moon

27 Wednesday
Libra • VOC (13h 22m)

Waxing Gibbous Moon

28 Thursday
VOC • Scorpio

Waxing Gibbous Moon

29 Friday
Scorpio

Waxing Gibbous Moon

May 2026

Journalling and Notes

30 Saturday
Scorpio • VOC (12h 41m) • Sagittarius

Waxing Gibbous Moon Phase ends

31 Sunday
Sagittarius • VOC (35h 59m)

Full Moon - Blue Moon - 09°55' Sagittarius

Desires, Goals and Intentions for June 2026

Welcome to June 2026

June 2026. Personal Choices and Positive Transformation!

June is a month when personal choice through awareness is definitely the name of the game!

The overall astro-dynamics bring an interesting mix of both positivity and forward motion... and possible challenge... and opportunity for reflection, hindsight, and learning from the past! It is as though the retrograde influences that bring reflection... alongside the massive turning point of the Solstices, that invite us to overcome challenges, both past and present... alongside some powerful planetary collaborations that bring a forward motion thrust of energy loaded with promise and opportunities for new beginnings... all combine!

At times the overall energy feels quite pressured, but through hindsight, self-responsibility, and awareness of our choices, this brings opportunity for awakening and much needed transformation, and whether this is internally in our attitudes and perceptions... or in the context of our immediate lives... or in global matters that affect us as a collective... how we respond to this mix is down to individual personal choice.

Our first card of Synchronicity aligning with Hagalaz, the Rune of Disruption is a reminder that everything happens with purpose... so even if something unexpected shows up or something that we thought was permanent seems to have passed its sell by date and longer serves us, this will be purposeful... life is always evolving and growing...

And our second card of Miracles acknowledges that miracles come in many different shapes and sizes... which aligning with Ehwaz, the Rune of Movement, confirms that whatever is happening around you, it is leading to the bettering of any situation, and how you respond and therefore how you influence the outcome is a personal choice.

Cards and Runes June 2026

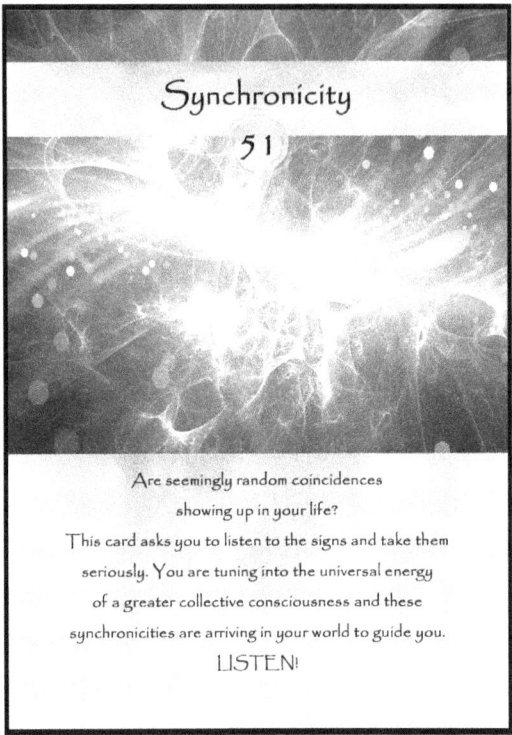

Cards and Runes June 2026

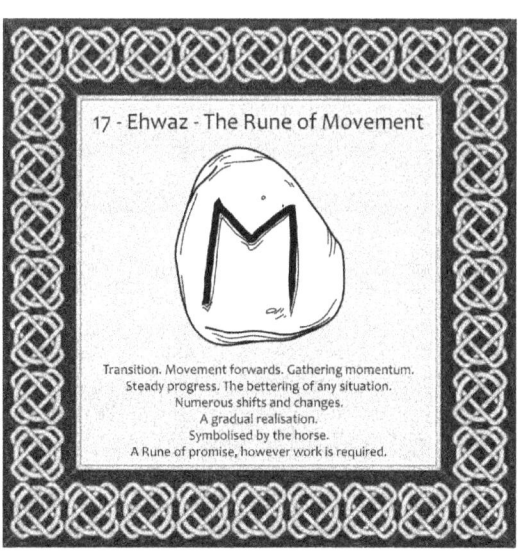

Moon Phases June 2026

The Disseminating or Waning Gibbous Moon – from 1 June to 7 June passing through Sagittarius, Capricorn, Aquarius, and into Pisces

The first couple of days of this Moon time feels quite steady and productive... so use this time well. The planetary collaborations then suggest the potential for some more challenging energetics that could lead to misunderstandings or misperceptions... and this flow of energy could escalate quite quickly or arrive unexpectedly. However, productivity and the potential for resolution then returns with a lovely underlying flavour of karmic possibilities... so if any hiccups occur in your world around the 3rd 4th or 5th ... try to be still and observe and process what is taking place... the planets will soon align to bring higher minded solutions and resolutions of higher purpose, bringing opportunities to push through these difficulties in ways that are beneficial for all.

The Last Quarter Moon – 8 June – 17°38' Pisces

The energetics of this Last Quarter Moon call us to remember that thoughts create things, and that you are the source of change within your world... and that your thoughts reach out further and beyond yourself and into the collective field.
This Moon invites you to take ownership of your deepest desires and acknowledge the aspects of your world, both inner and outer... personally and globally... where you wish to see change... and then shift your focus and the power of your thoughts to the future that you wish to create. So often we dwell in the energy of what isn't right or what we don't have... rather than the potential solution and the essence of what we desire. Use this Moon time to review and evaluate and take an ownership of the power of your mind to create the world that you wish to see.

The Balsamic Moon or Waning Crescent Moon – from 9 June to 14 June passing from Pisces, and through Aries, Taurus, and Gemini

The Last Quarter invited you to take charge of your thoughts and bring your focus to what you want to see, create and manifest, and this Moon phase now invites you to follow through with actions. The overall astro-dynamics suggest an underlying edge of hard work, and a time when perhaps tough conversations might need to be had, either with ourselves or with others... on the one hand, the energetics support us in confronting our deepest fears and committing to working through these to reach positive outcomes... on the other hand, resistance to change or a determination to cling to what no longer serves may also be present. Our beautiful Moon does her best to soften these energies and as this Moon time progresses the overall flow of energy lightens up, suggesting the potential to navigate through and beyond difficulties and find valuable solutions.

 ### The Super New Moon – 15 June – 24°03' Gemini

Self-mastery is key to humanity's evolution to higher levels of consciousness, and the astro-dynamics of today's Super New Moon in Gemini invite a day of pause. Amidst the intensity of overall accelerated growth, this Moon asks us each to hold 'the Eagles perch' position and observe from all sides and all angles… dwelling in the past and holding on to grievances will not create a future of peace, balance, and harmony… however, learning from the past and with a dedicated commitment to ensure that mistakes are not repeated, can bring about a future that honours equality, fairness, and respect, not only for one another but for all of life, including our beautiful planet, and we each have our part to play in this. So use today to set wishes and intentions that honour your own uniqueness, but also your part in the shared collective of the future that is being created right now.

New Moon Global Timings:
Los Angeles, USA	Sun, 14 Jun 2026 at 19:53 PDT
New York, USA	Sun, 14 Jun 2026 at 22:53 EDT
Reykjavik, Iceland	Mon, 15 Jun 2026 at 02:53 GMT
London, UK	Mon, 15 Jun 2026 at 03:53 BST
Paris, France	Mon, 15 Jun 2026 at 04:53 CEST
Cape Town, SA	Mon, 15 Jun 2026 at 04:53 SAST
Delhi, India	Mon, 15 Jun 2026 at 08:23 IST
Perth, Australia	Mon, 15 Jun 2026 at 10:53 AWST
Tokyo, Japan	Mon, 15 Jun 2026 at 11:53 JST
Sydney, Australia	Mon, 15 Jun 2026 at 12:53 AEST
Auckland, NZ	Mon, 15 Jun 2026 at 14:53 NZST
GMT/UTC	Mon, 15 Jun 2026 at 02:53 GMT

 ### The Waxing Crescent Moon – from 16 June to 20 June – passing through Cancer, Leo, and Virgo

The flow of energy during this Moon time can be roughly divided into two halves. In the first half… despite offering the potential for progression and forward motion, this period gets off to a slightly bumpy start… but don't be discouraged! The four day window that surrounds the summer solstice in the Northern Hemisphere and the winter solstice in the Southern Hemisphere is a pivotal shift in the Earths calendar and often heralds a time when a significant surge of growth is indicated, and in the second half, as we move towards the Solstice, the energy is surprisingly flowing, suggesting transition, movement, and change. The overall dynamics also seem to shift the emphasis of our focus from the outer world and global events to the immediacy of our own personal environment, including our immediate relationships, so whatever is taking place within the immediacy of your world, embrace every opportunity for transformation and the universe will be right behind you!

 ### The First Quarter Moon – 21 June – 00°32' Libra

Having a First Quarter Moon on the Solstice is pretty magical! Energetically, we don't always get such a beautifully aligned opportunity... and this Moon is sitting right on the Earth's axis... adding massive weight to the energy of today!
A First Quarter Moon naturally invites evaluation and review, promising to show exactly what is needed to make progression and growth possible... and the dynamics today are incredibly favourable and flowing, suggesting movement forwards with harmony and with balance, and with an added potential for massive spiritual downloads! So make the most of this incredible day and open yourself to receive whatever guidance you need in any area of your world.

 ### The Waxing Gibbous Moon – from 22 June to 29 June passing through Libra, Scorpio, and Sagittarius

Initially this Moon phase feels very free flowing, however this rapidly intensifies, bringing an overall energy flow that feels dynamic, fast-paced, emotionally sensitive, and potentially a bit up and down... and although the overall planetary alignments suggest a ton of positive possibilities, it may also be difficult to feel anchored or keep realistic perspectives, given the pace and changeability of the overall dynamics. We are now full into the Mercury retrograde shadow and so whatever is happening in your world, try to keep your feet firmly on the ground and think of this Moon time as an opportunity to try things out and to see what feels right and what doesn't... this can then lead to realistic choices that are rooted in awareness. Just before the Full Moon the energy lightens up suggesting increased clarity and potential breakthroughs.

 ### The Full Moon – 30 June – 08°14' Capricorn

Today Mercury moves into a retrograde period lasting until July 23rd and when a planet 'stations direct'... (this is the exact point of turn) the retrograde energy and all of the planetary connections are significantly intensified and strengthened! Now today's Full Moon is inviting healing, and in a big way... so don't be surprised if something from the past returns, or if events, situations, and circumstances cause you to slow down... or to look back or reflect... or simply to re-evaluate. The purpose is to help you to realign and if necessary, to heal, and to shed, cleanse, and release… or at the very least, to take some time out and come back replenished.

The overall dynamics of our beautiful Moon suggest the potential for some profound moments of awareness today and as always, a Full Moon often brings insights and illumination, so if at all possible, approach today at a snail's pace and simply be present to whatever shows up.

Full Moon Global Timings:
Los Angeles, USA	Mon, 29 Jun 2026 at 16:56 PDT
New York, USA	Mon, 29 Jun 2026 at 19:56 EDT
Reykjavik, Iceland	Mon, 29 Jun 2026 at 23:56 GMT
London, UK	Tue, 30 Jun 2026 at 00:56 BST
Paris, France	Tue, 30 Jun 2026 at 01:56 CEST
Cape Town, SA	Tue, 30 Jun 2026 at 01:56 SAST
Delhi, India	Tue, 30 Jun 2026 at 05:26 IST
Perth, Australia	Tue, 30 Jun 2026 at 07:56 AWST
Tokyo, Japan	Tue, 30 Jun 2026 at 08:56 JST
Sydney, Australia	Tue, 30 Jun 2026 at 09:56 AEST
Auckland, NZ	Tue, 30 Jun 2026 at 11:56 NZST
GMT/UTC	Mon, 29 Jun 2026 at 23:56 GMT

June 2026

1   Monday

VOC

Waning Gibbous Moon Phase starts
Mercury Enters Cancer

2   Tuesday

VOC • Capricorn

Waning Gibbous Moon

3   Wednesday

Capricorn

Waning Gibbous Moon

4   Thursday

Capricorn • VOC (10h 43m) • Aquarius

Waning Gibbous Moon

5   Friday

Aquarius • VOC (28h 53m)

Waning Gibbous Moon

June 2026

Journalling and Notes

6   Saturday
VOC

Waning Gibbous Moon

7   Sunday
VOC • Pisces

Waning Gibbous Moon Phase ends

June 2026

8 Monday

Pisces

Last Quarter Moon 17°38' Pisces

9 Tuesday

Pisces • VOC (7h 56m) • Aries

Waning Crescent Moon Phase starts

10 Wednesday

Aries

Waning Crescent Moon

11 Thursday

Aries • VOC (4h 7m) • Taurus

Waning Crescent Moon

12 Friday

Taurus

Waning Crescent Moon

June 2026

Journalling and Notes

---

13 Saturday

Taurus • VOC (5h 37m) • Gemini

Waning Crescent Moon
Venus Enters Leo

14 Sunday

Gemini

Waning Crescent Moon Phase ends

June 2026

15 Monday
Gemini • VOC (9h 21m) • Cancer

Super New Moon 24°03' Gemini

16 Tuesday
Cancer

Waxing Crescent Moon Phase starts

17 Wednesday
Cancer • VOC (4h 25m) • Leo

Waxing Crescent Moon

18 Thursday
Leo

Waxing Crescent Moon

19 Friday
Leo • VOC (3h 7m) • Virgo

Waxing Crescent Moon
Chiron Enters Taurus
Juneteenth – USA

June 2026

Journalling and Notes

20 Saturday
Virgo

Waxing Crescent Moon Phase ends

21 Sunday
Virgo • VOC (3h 23m) • Libra

First Quarter Moon 00°32' Libra
Sun Enters Cancer
Summer Solstice Northern Hemisphere – Winter Solstice Southern Hemisphere

June 2026

22 Monday
Libra

Waxing Gibbous Moon Phase starts

23 Tuesday
Libra

Waxing Gibbous Moon

24 Wednesday
Libra • VOC (2h 34m) • Scorpio

Waxing Gibbous Moon

25 Thursday
Scorpio

Waxing Gibbous Moon

26 Friday
Scorpio • VOC (1h 32m) • Sagittarius

Waxing Gibbous Moon

June 2026

Journalling and Notes

---

27 Saturday
Sagittarius

Waxing Gibbous Moon

28 Sunday
Sagittarius • VOC (26h 15m)

Waxing Gibbous Moon

Desires, Goals and Intentions for July 2026

Welcome to July 2026

July 2026. Evolutionary Progression, Divine Timing, and Self-Mastery!

The energies of July are powerful and dynamic and support progression with a distinct overall flavour of karmic inevitability and divine timing... Now if everything in your world is geared for change and transformation the energies of this month could really be working for you... but if you've got a lot going on and you'd just like to slow down or even stop completely, then this month could prove to be a little challenging... the key here is to recognise that the universal energy is shifting and changing and fast... and to consciously align with this.

Our first card of Open Yourself to Possibility aligning with Wunjo, the Rune of Joy, validates the extraordinary potential that is currently available for us whilst also validating that the outcome of any potential transformation will be favourable... in many ways this card and Rune acknowledge that the universe most definitely has the upper hand and that any upheaval that is currently taking place is arriving with divine timing to create powerfully positive possibilities!

Our second card of Self-Care invites you to recognise and take responsibility for your personal needs during this period of powerful accelerated growth. Aligning with Thurisaz the Rune of Gateway, which calls you to pause and reflect before stepping forwards with conscious awareness, this combination highlights the incredible levels of personal empowerment that we can develop through heightened levels of self-awareness. This card and Rune also invite you to reflect upon your part in the bigger picture!

On an energetic level, our individual thoughts, words, deeds, and actions, all play a part in shaping the evolutionary transformations of our times... and this level of conscious awareness is an integral part of humanities overall expansion... so embrace the flow of change but be sure to reflect along the way!

Cards and Runes July 2026

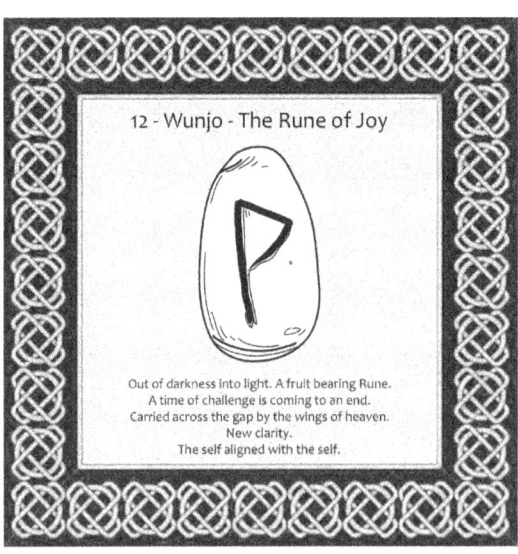

Cards and Runes July 2026

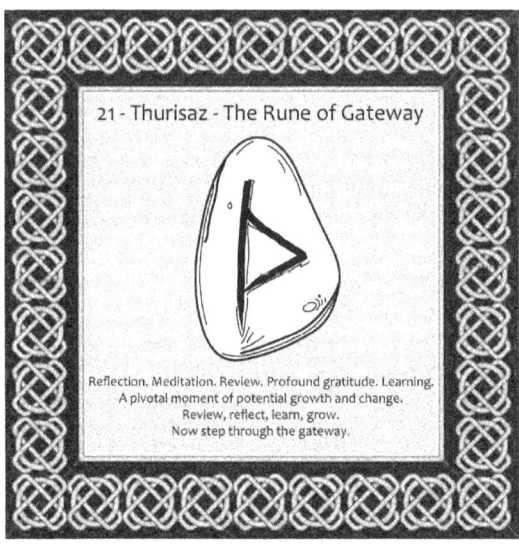

Moon Phases July 2026

 The Disseminating or Waning Gibbous Moon – from 1 July to 6 July passing through Capricorn, Aquarius, Pisces, and into Aries

Following the illuminations of the Full Moon that emphasised the need for healing, this Moon time follows through with an emphasis on rebirth, transformation, and healing. It is almost as though the current retrograde energies bring the past into focus in such a way that the need for change and indeed healing, cannot be denied… and this is accompanied by some incredibly strong and yest profoundly positive planetary collaborations that hold open windows of energetic opportunity so we can initiate the changes that are needed. There is also an interesting flavour of fate and destiny towards the end of this Moon time suggesting divine timing with an energy that pushes impatiently for change!

 The Last Quarter Moon – 7 July – 15°41' Aries

The dynamics of today's Last Quarter Moon arrive with a very distinct flavour of realism… and yet also hold a dreamy space of possibilities. In the previous Moon time, the energies were pushing for movement… and now this Moon invites you to reflect and to hold an optimistic view of the future and all that is possible, and yet also be grounded and real about what is achievable. Held in balance, these energies are a fabulous combination to lean into…. and so, if for whatever reason you find yourself swinging too far in either direction… either overly dreamy and optimistic but without a strong anchor point… or so firmly anchored that you feel stuck… the energy today creates a wonderful window of time when you can realign and rebalance.

 The Balsamic Moon or Waning Crescent Moon – from 8 July to 13 July passing through Aries, Taurus, Gemini, and Cancer

Overall, the prevailing energy of this Moon phase is one of positivity, and although there are some spikes of more intense energy, these will most likely be arriving to give you a nudge in the best direction for you. In the middle of this period the Moon collaborates with some significant planetary dynamics that suggest the potential for profound insights, spiritual downloads, and unexpected or out-of-the-box solutions… and this is followed by an energetic suggesting circumstances that might push you to want to act upon your new levels of awareness… however, please remember that not everyone will be on the same page… and given the current retrograde energies, it may be beneficial to gather your thoughts and take some time to reflect and contemplate before taking any immediate or direct actions.

The Super New Moon – 14 July – 21°59' Cancer (see VOC Moons p.212)

The magnetism of this Super New Moon is enhanced by her close proximity to the Earth… and the exact timing of this Moon aligns with a huge 13-hour Void of Course period.
There is also a dynamic today that suggests the desire to break free from restrictions or aspects of your life where you have felt held back. Now this energy could feel incredibly liberating… but it could also leave you feeling a bit at out at sea… but with full awareness of this, you can actually use the energy to its fullest potential. So use this Moon time to consciously focus on wishes and intentions that liberate you from anything that holds you back… and then ask for the beautiful nurturing energy of Cancer to bring the fertility needed to nurture your dreams and wishes into form.

New Moon Global Timings:
Los Angeles, USA	Tue, 14 Jul 2026 at 02:43 PDT
New York, USA	Tue, 14 Jul 2026 at 05:43 EDT
Reykjavik, Iceland	Tue, 14 Jul 2026 at 09:43 GMT
London, UK	Tue, 14 Jul 2026 at 10:43 BST
Paris, France	Tue, 14 Jul 2026 at 11:43 CEST
Cape Town, SA	Tue, 14 Jul 2026 at 11:43 SAST
Delhi, India	Tue, 14 Jul 2026 at 15:13 IST
Perth, Australia	Tue, 14 Jul 2026 at 17:43 AWST
Tokyo, Japan	Tue, 14 Jul 2026 at 18:43 JST
Sydney, Australia	Tue, 14 Jul 2026 at 19:43 AEST
Auckland, NZ	Tue, 14 Jul 2026 at 21:43 NZST
GMT/UTC	Tue, 14 Jul 2026 at 09:43 GMT

 The Waxing Crescent Moon – from 15 July to 20 July – passing through Leo, Virgo, and Libra

This flow of energy in this Moon time is powerful and in a really positive way! The energy gets going easily… and it has flow and impetus, and the momentum just keeps on growing! Rather like driving a car from a stationary position straight out onto a road… you accelerate gently and without hinderance the car just gathers in speed… and the energy also suggests events running with karmic precision! There are some stronger undertones, particularly towards the end of this Moon time, and we are still in the midst of some significant retrograde dynamics… but the overall essence is fuelling enhanced growth… so even if interruptions or a delay occurs it will almost certainly arrive to facilitate some form of accelerated growth!

The First Quarter Moon – 21 July – 28°43' Libra

A First Quarter Moon is traditionally thought to bring opportunities to evaluate, and usually in response to external events and circumstances. Today our beautiful Moon teams up with some incredibly powerful planetary alignments, pushing for expansion and rebirth… and on a big scale! And although this is not without potential tension, this is balanced by other major planetary collaborations that bring a very flowing energy that also desires expansion and re-birth… and also in a big way! So this will be an interesting time… both individually and on the global stage. But whatever is happening in your world, if transformation and change through conscious choice are on your agenda… then the energies today are backing you 100%.

 ### The Waxing Gibbous Moon – from 22 July to 28 July passing through Scorpio, Sagittarius, and Capricorn

The planetary collaborations of this Moon phase hold an incredibly strong and profoundly positive dynamic throughout, and as our beautiful Moon, gathers in strength she feeds and fuels this potential.
As she passes through Scorpio, Sagittarius, and then into Capricorn, you may well feel the potential of this energy shift through different stages of development… from a space of deep introspection with issues that were previously unknown or below the surface coming to light… which in turn creates a space of possibility through awareness… which then leads to constructive planning and an opportunity to take actions that bring genuine progress… whether personal or on the global stage, it is as though the Universe is paving the way for evolutionary progression!

 ### The Full Moon – 29 July – 06°30' Aquarius

The energies of this Full Moon are something else! On the one hand there are huge expansive energetics fuelling and expanding, change and rebirth… on the other hand there are underlying tensions that could create some sparks…
Now if these are sparks of passion then all well and good… but if underlying frustrations have not been recognised or voiced this is a Moon that could bring them to the surface and with velocity.
The Lunar influence also links with some profoundly spiritual dimensions that promise new opportunities and higher visions, and these channels of higher-minded insight could arrive unexpectedly and yet offer keys and solutions to enable changes to flow easily and fluently into our lives… wow… watch this space!

Full Moon Global Timings:

Los Angeles, USA	Wed, 29 Jul 2026 at 07:35 PDT
New York, USA	Wed, 29 Jul 2026 at 10:35 EDT
Reykjavik, Iceland	Wed, 29 Jul 2026 at 14:35 GMT
London, UK	Wed, 29 Jul 2026 at 15:35 BST
Paris, France	Wed, 29 Jul 2026 at 16:35 CEST
Cape Town, SA	Wed, 29 Jul 2026 at 16:35 SAST
Delhi, India	Wed, 29 Jul 2026 at 20:05 IST
Perth, Australia	Wed, 29 Jul 2026 at 22:35 AWST
Tokyo, Japan	Wed, 29 Jul 2026 at 23:35 JST
Sydney, Australia	Thu, 30 Jul 2026 at 00:35 AEST
Auckland, NZ	Thu, 30 Jul 2026 at 02:35 NZST
GMT/UTC	Wed, 29 Jul 2026 at 14:35 GMT

The Disseminating or Waning Gibbous Moon – from 30 July to 5 August passing through Aquarius, Pisces, Aries, and into Taurus

Throughout this Moon time an underlying tension remains, coming in waves, with some stronger than others, and these dynamics could fuel powerfully positive passions, but also some more challenging emotions. Fortunately, the overall astro-dynamics are equally promoting positive transformation through higher vision, and early on, when our beautiful Moon passes from Aquarius into Pisces, the Lunar influence taps into a distinctly Karmic essence followed by a delightful burst of healing. Now depending on your unique personal circumstances, the influence of this period could vary considerably, but the spiritual dynamics emphasise self-mastery through awareness, so at all times be conscious of your personal choice!

June / July 2026

29 Monday
VOC • Capricorn

Waxing Gibbous Moon Phase ends
Mercury Retrograde Begins

30 Tuesday
Capricorn

Full Moon 08°14' Capricorn
Jupiter Enters Leo

1 Wednesday
Capricorn • VOC (7h 43m) • Aquarius

Waning Gibbous Moon Phase starts

2 Thursday
Aquarius

Waning Gibbous Moon

3 Friday
Aquarius • VOC (13h 3m)

Waning Gibbous Moon

July 2026

Journalling and Notes

4 Saturday
VOC • Pisces

Waning Gibbous Moon
Independence Day - USA

5 Sunday
Pisces

Waning Gibbous Moon

July 2026

6 Monday

Pisces • VOC (9h 47m) • Aries

Waning Gibbous Moon Phase ends

---

7 Tuesday

Aries

Last Quarter Moon 15°41' Aries
Neptune Retrograde Begins

---

8 Wednesday

Aries • VOC (1h 50m) • Taurus

Waning Crescent Moon Phase starts

---

9 Thursday

Taurus

Waning Crescent Moon
Venus Enters Virgo

---

10 Friday

Taurus • VOC (12h 30m)

Waning Crescent Moon
Matariki Day – Holiday NZ

July 2026

Journalling and Notes

---

11 Saturday
VOC • Gemini

Waning Crescent Moon

---

12 Sunday
Gemini • VOC (24h 36m)

Waning Crescent Moon

July 2026

13 Monday
VOC • Cancer

Waning Crescent Moon Phase ends

14 Tuesday
Cancer • VOC (12h 52m)

Super New Moon 21°59' Cancer

15 Wednesday
VOC • Leo

Waxing Crescent Moon Phase starts

16 Thursday
Leo • VOC (25h 41m)

Waxing Crescent Moon

17 Friday
VOC • Virgo

Waxing Crescent Moon

July 2026

Journalling and Notes

---

18 Saturday

Virgo

Waxing Crescent Moon

---

19 Sunday

Virgo • VOC (6h 45m) • Libra

Waxing Crescent Moon

July 2026

20 Monday
Libra

Waxing Crescent Moon Phase ends

21 Tuesday
Libra • VOC (2h 30m) • Scorpio

First Quarter Moon 28°43' Libra

22 Wednesday
Scorpio • VOC (27h 19m)

Waxing Gibbous Moon Phase starts
Sun Enters Leo

23 Thursday
VOC

Waxing Gibbous Moon

24 Friday
VOC • Sagittarius

Waxing Gibbous Moon
Mercury Retrograde Ends

July 2026

Journalling and Notes

25 Saturday
Sagittarius • VOC (22h 47m)

Waxing Gibbous Moon

26 Sunday
VOC • Capricorn

Waxing Gibbous Moon
Saturn Retrograde Begins

July 2026

27 Monday
Capricorn

Waxing Gibbous Moon

28 Tuesday
Capricorn • VOC (19h 36m)

Waxing Gibbous Moon Phase ends

29 Wednesday
VOC • Aquarius

Full Moon 06°30' Aquarius

30 Thursday
Aquarius • VOC (14h 48m)

Waning Gibbous Moon Phase starts

31 Friday
VOC • Pisces

Waning Gibbous Moon

August 2026

Journalling and Notes

---

1   Saturday

Pisces

Waning Gibbous Moon
Festivals of Lammas Northern Hemisphere – Imbolc Southern Hemisphere

---

2   Sunday

Pisces • VOC (8h 5m) • Aries

Waning Gibbous Moon

Desires, Goals and Intentions for August 2026

Welcome to August 2026

August 2026. Welcome to Eclipse Season… A Time of Stepping Up!

In comparison to the previous month of July, the astro energetics this month suggest an interesting shift in the flavour of the energy… on one hand the astrology still feels very dynamic, however there is also an undertone that suggests we can link with a greater sense of strength and resilience… it is as if the seeds that were sown in July not only germinate, but begin to take root.

Our first card of Leadership invites us each to step up and to recognise that we all lead by example… so whatever is taking place in your world, even though the overall flow of energy is still quite full on and potentially fast paced, there is also opportunity to consolidate growth. With Wunjo the Rune of Joy, showing up for a second month in a row, it really highlights the phenomenal positive potentials that are now emerging and can begin to take shape!

Regardless of what is happening, either globally or in the context of your own unique personal circumstances, August is a month when we are collectively invited to really think about where and how we wish to invest our energy, and because we are in Eclipse season there is a profound opportunity to observe the way that past actions have created the shape of NOW and use the wisdom of hindsight to consciously create the shape of the future that we wish to see.

Our second card of Which Direction reinforces the power of personal choice in the present moment as well as acknowledging that when we learn from every experience there is always a positive outcome to be found. Joined by Ansuz the Rune of Signs and Signals, which resonates perfectly with the karmic nature of the Eclipse energy this is definitely a month to own your own sovereignty and be very aware of how and where you invest your energy.

Cards and Runes August 2026

Cards and Runes August 2026

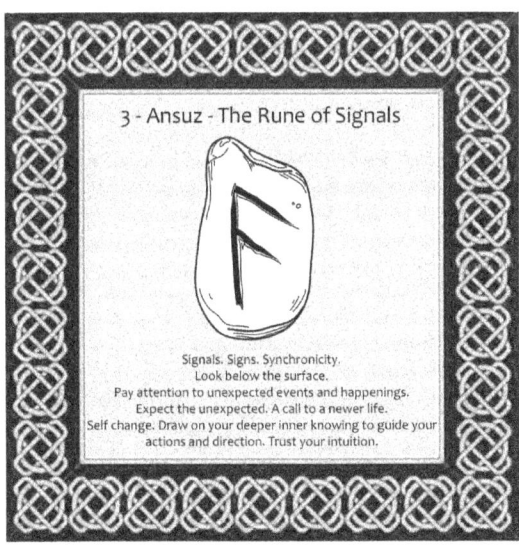

Moon Phases August 2026

 The Disseminating or Waning Gibbous Moon – from 30 July to 5 August passing through Aquarius, Pisces, Aries, and into Taurus

Throughout this Moon time an underlying tension remains, coming in waves, with some stronger than others, and these dynamics could fuel powerfully positive passions, but also some more challenging emotions. Fortunately, the overall astro-dynamics are equally promoting positive transformation through higher vision, and early on, when our beautiful Moon passes from Aquarius into Pisces, the Lunar influence taps into a distinctly Karmic essence followed by a delightful burst of healing. Now depending on your unique personal circumstances, the influence of this period could vary considerably, but the spiritual dynamics emphasise self-mastery through awareness, so at all times be conscious of your personal choice!

 The Last Quarter Moon – 6 August – 13°40' Taurus

Todays Last Quarter Moon brings a buoyant energy suggesting the potential for confident, and even bold actions, however additional dynamics also point to an interesting duality. The energetics offer a wonderful flow of creative inspiration, however within this flow there could also be the potential for some over idealisation, or an overly inflated sense of expectation, which could in turn lead to feelings of disillusionment if something doesn't then work out. The Last Quarter influence emphasises personal responsibility, inviting action through conscious reflective self-awareness… so lean into the positivity of the day… but slow down and evaluate realistically before taking action.

 The Balsamic Moon or Waning Crescent Moon – from 7 August to 11 August passing through Gemini, Cancer, and Leo

Following the exuberance of the Last Quarter Moon, the energetics of this Moon time suggest the opportunity for some solid reality testing! Initially, the energy flows easily so enjoy this pocket of time and use it to either progress with ease or to smooth out any immediate tensions that you may need to deal with. As this Moon phase progresses the astro-dynamics heat up with the potential for a clash between desires and realistic expectations, with possible discord in communications either with others, or within yourself. However, despite these tensions, a powerfully positive energetic governs this entire period supporting growth and resolution through open communications that through acknowledgment and validation can create a balanced outcome. And as always… how this emerges within our own personal circumstances is down to us each… the energy is what it is… and what we do with it is our personal choice.

The New Moon Total Solar Eclipse – 12 August – 20°01' Leo (See Eclipse Moons p.213)

Given the overall themes of the previous Moon phases, today the dynamics are loaded with promise and exciting possibilities, although these possibilities may not arrive in predictable circumstances! Within the planetary alignments there are two strong Kite formations, which bring an extremely auspicious energy of openings and massive potential… alongside this, the energy of Eclipse Season is said to create a portal that enables you to plug into the timeline that connects the past, the present, and the future showing you how actions and events in the past have contributed to your present circumstances, with an opportunity to step into your own sovereignty and make clear conscious choices and changes in the here and now to shape and create the future you wish to see. Today is a powerful window of personal opportunity so be sure to set clear wishes and intentions and be prepared to follow them through with tangible actions.

New Moon Global Timings:
Los Angeles, USA	Wed, 12 Aug 2026 at 10:36 PDT
New York, USA	Wed, 12 Aug 2026 at 13:36 EDT
Reykjavik, Iceland	Wed, 12 Aug 2026 at 17:36 GMT
London, UK	Wed, 12 Aug 2026 at 18:36 BST
Paris, France	Wed, 12 Aug 2026 at 19:36 CEST
Cape Town, SA	Wed, 12 Aug 2026 at 19:36 SAST
Delhi, India	Wed, 12 Aug 2026 at 23:06 IST
Perth, Australia	Thu, 13 Aug 2026 at 01:36 AWST
Tokyo, Japan	Thu, 13 Aug 2026 at 02:36 JST
Sydney, Australia	Thu, 13 Aug 2026 at 03:36 AEST
Auckland, NZ	Thu, 13 Aug 2026 at 05:36 NZST
GMT/UTC	Wed, 12 Aug 2026 at 17:36 GMT

 The Waxing Crescent Moon – from 13 August to 19 August – passing through Virgo, Libra, and Scorpio

The Karmic qualities of Eclipse season dominate the start of this Moon time with the Lunar energy in full flow suggesting solid and genuine progress so in existing projects you should be able to move things forwards and in any new ventures get started with ease. Consistent, diligent, and steady actions will pay dividends with the added bonus of potentially divinely timed connections arriving that support your progress 100%. When the Moon enters Libra we see some far stronger energies at play coming in surges, and these waves of strong energy continue throughout this Moon phase, so if you find your flow is in any way disrupted or you find yourself losing focus, trust that there will be purpose to this… perhaps something needs to be tweaked or course corrected?

The First Quarter Moon – 20 August – 27°07' Scorpio

A First Quarter Moon is Always a point of evaluation and this Moon links with an energy of powerful Karmic potential! Overall, the astrodynamics are immensely positive, suggesting the potential to receive significant downloads of insight that bring both clarity of mind in your internal thoughts… and clarity of direction in your external world. This feels like a powerful day of Divine timing when the Lunar influence may well highlight your calling or your purpose… or at the very least, highlight where you are on track, and where you are not! So, if at all possible, make space today to have stillness breaks and consciously create pockets of time for meditation and open yourself to receive guidance.

 ### The Waxing Gibbous Moon – from 21 August to 27 August passing through Sagittarius, Capricorn, Aquarius, and into Pisces

Following such profound and eye opening dynamics at the First Quarter Moon, right at the start of this Moon phase the Lunar influence suggests the potential for some unexpected upheaval or shake ups, and this could be in your internal perceptions, or your external circumstances, however the upheaval should be should be fleeting and the overall energetics move very quickly into more harmonious collaborations that promise a continual flow of steady growth and progression… and our Moon adds weight to this! The overall flavour of this Moon time suggests that new ways of seeing, being, and doing, can really begin to take shape and solidify… and even though there are some undertones of tension throughout, the positivity of the more flowing planetary collaborations way outweighs these energies, so use this time well and enjoy!

 ### The Full Moon Partial Lunar Eclipse – 28 August – 04°54' Pisces (See Eclipse Moons p.213)

Today's Full Moon Eclipse in deeply spiritual Pisces is not only auspicious but also suggests Divine Timing! Our beautiful Moon creates a powerful karmic collaboration and directly opens channels of communication… and there is also a powerful planetary connection that suggests unexpected happenings that are specifically designed to wake us up and bring about change… and fast! So, expect the unexpected… and whatever this Moon brings for you today, the energetics are literally opening you to the infinite possibilities that sit within the dreamtime! This is a day when Source/Spirit/the Universe takes the lead and potentially opens the way for you to see what you need to see to step into your highest potential… and this could be a way bigger picture than you had previously imagined… so take time to dream today!

Full Moon Global Timings:

Los Angeles, USA	Thu, 27 Aug 2026 at 21:18 PDT
New York, USA	Fri, 28 Aug 2026 at 00:18 EDT
Reykjavik, Iceland	Fri, 28 Aug 2026 at 04:18 GMT
London, UK	Fri, 28 Aug 2026 at 05:18 BST
Paris, France	Fri, 28 Aug 2026 at 06:18 CEST
Cape Town, SA	Fri, 28 Aug 2026 at 06:18 SAST
Delhi, India	Fri, 28 Aug 2026 at 09:48 IST
Perth, Australia	Fri, 28 Aug 2026 at 12:18 AWST
Tokyo, Japan	Fri, 28 Aug 2026 at 13:18 JST
Sydney, Australia	Fri, 28 Aug 2026 at 14:18 AEST
Auckland, NZ	Fri, 28 Aug 2026 at 16:18 NZST
GMT/UTC	Fri, 28 Aug 2026 at 04:18 GMT

The Disseminating or Waning Gibbous Moon – from 29 August to 3 September passing through Pisces, Aries, Taurus, and into Gemini

As our beautiful Moon begins this phase the energy suddenly intensifies, and although this is brief it is also significant with an undertone of divine timing and Karmic potential… so notice and observe. We then see three very distinct stages of Lunar flow… firstly there are several days of more gentle steadying energy… however as the Moon moves through Aries and Taurus the energetics intensify again, suggesting some push pull energy where you might want to take action and yet the timing may not be quite right… and then at the end of this Moon phase the energy flows easily again… so whatever is happening in your world try to be conscious of these different shifts in pace and speed and use them to your advantage.

August 2026

3 Monday
Aries

Waning Gibbous Moon
Chiron Retrograde Begins

4 Tuesday
Aries • VOC (7h 45m)

Waning Gibbous Moon

5 Wednesday
VOC • Taurus

Waning Gibbous Moon Phase ends

6 Thursday
Taurus

Last Quarter Moon 13°40' Taurus
Venus Enters Libra

7 Friday
Taurus • VOC (6h 44m) • Gemini

Waning Crescent Moon Phase starts

August 2026

Journalling and Notes

---

8 Saturday
Gemini

Waning Crescent Moon

---

9 Sunday
Gemini • VOC (2h 20m) • Cancer

Waning Crescent Moon
Mercury Enters Leo
United Nations Indigenous Peoples Day

August 2026

---

10 Monday

Cancer • VOC (25h 8m)

Waning Crescent Moon

---

11 Tuesday

VOC • Leo

Waning Crescent Moon Phase ends
Mars Enters Cancer

---

12 Wednesday

Leo • VOC (16h 42m)

New Moon Total Solar Eclipse 20°01' Leo

---

13 Thursday

VOC • Virgo • VOC (42h 57m)

Waxing Crescent Moon Phase starts

---

14 Friday

VOC

Waxing Crescent Moon

August 2026

Journalling and Notes

15 Saturday
VOC • Libra

Waxing Crescent Moon

16 Sunday
Libra

Waxing Crescent Moon

August 2026

17 Monday
Libra • VOC (10h 16m) • Scorpio

Waxing Crescent Moon

18 Tuesday
Scorpio

Waxing Crescent Moon
Nodes leave Pisces and Virgo

19 Wednesday
Scorpio

Waxing Crescent Moon Phase ends

20 Thursday
Scorpio • VOC (5h 44m) • Sagittarius

First Quarter Moon 27°07' Scorpio

21 Friday
Sagittarius

Waxing Gibbous Moon Phase starts

August 2026

Journalling and Notes

22 Saturday
Sagittarius • VOC (29m) • Capricorn

Waxing Gibbous Moon

23 Sunday
Capricorn

Waxing Gibbous Moon
Sun Enters Virgo

August 2026

24 Monday
Capricorn • VOC (26h 33m)

Waxing Gibbous Moon

25 Tuesday
VOC • Aquarius

Waxing Gibbous Moon
Mercury Enters Virgo

26 Wednesday
Aquarius • VOC (21h 5m)

Waxing Gibbous Moon

27 Thursday
VOC • Pisces

Waxing Gibbous Moon Phase ends

28 Friday
Pisces • VOC (34h 25m)

Full Moon Partial Lunar Eclipse 04°54' Pisces

August 2026

Journalling and Notes

29 **Saturday**
VOC

Waning Gibbous Moon Phase starts

30 **Sunday**
VOC • Aries

Waning Gibbous Moon

Desires, Goals and Intentions for September 2026

Welcome to September 2026

September 2026... Testing your Ability to Consciously Manifest!

September brings a month when the overall astrodynamics invite us each to really think about the relationship between our thoughts and words... and our deeds and actions... and how these are actively creating the world around us.

At the start of the month, the Lunar influence feeds into some push/pull energy suggesting a need to evaluate... and this is reinforced by our first card of Course Correct that invites us to recognise that when something doesn't run smoothly or there are hiccups or delays it isn't necessarily a negative! This card aligns with Ehwaz, the Rune of Movement, which suggests shifts and changes and the gathering of momentum, with positive expansion and progression, and the bettering of any situation. Together they highlight the importance and the value of developing our ability to listen to events and circumstances as a source of guidance rather than a hinderance, enabling us to hold the higher perspective and manifest more consciously.

As the month progresses the overall astro-dynamics increase in intensity, suggesting the potential for some discordant energies in the overall planetary connections... however there are also some equally strong extremely positive dynamics suggesting the potential for resolution and healing... and so this is an interesting mix!

Our second card of Nurture, aligning with Mannaz, the Rune of the Self, asks us to focus on ourselves and the part that we each play in manifesting for the greater good... what are your thoughts, words, deeds and actions creating? The card of Nurture highlights the need to develop self-mastery through self-awareness suggesting that the astro-dynamics are best responded to through nurture and responsiveness rather than any form of re-action or impulsive or hasty decision making, with the Rune of the Self emphasising personal free will and conscious choice.

Cards and Runes September 2026

Cards and Runes September 2026

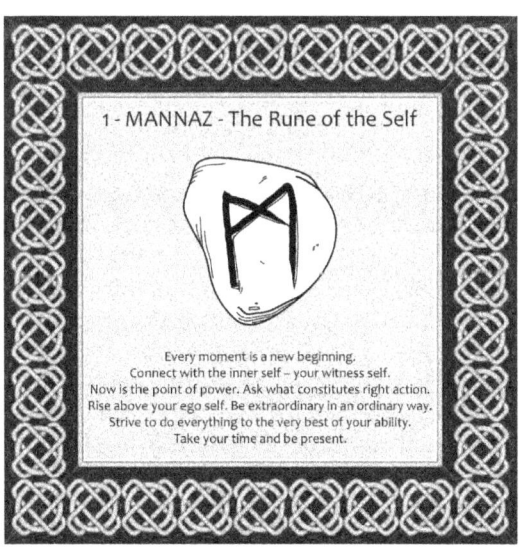

Moon Phases September 2026

 The Disseminating or Waning Gibbous Moon – from 29 August to 3 September passing through Pisces, Aries, Taurus, and into Gemini

As our beautiful Moon begins this phase the energy suddenly intensifies, and although this is brief it is also significant with an undertone of divine timing and Karmic potential… so notice and observe. We then see three very distinct stages of Lunar flow… firstly there are several days of more gentle steadying energy… however as the Moon moves through Aries and Taurus the energetics intensify again, suggesting some push pull energy where you might want to take action and yet the timing may not be quite right… and then at the end of this Moon phase the energy flows easily again… so whatever is happening in your world try to be conscious of these different shifts in pace and speed and use them to your advantage.

 The Last Quarter Moon – 4 September – 11°48' Gemini

Todays Last Quarter Moon Embodies a curious mix of predominantly positive dynamics whilst also bringing an additional flavour of the unexpected, with the potential for sudden or impulsive actions. Now all Quarter Moons naturally favour evaluation with the Last Quarter Moon influence inspiring you to step up and to be your authentic self… and one of the strongest of the many positive influences today invites auspicious communications and conversations! Given this mix the energetics today could open some exciting, new or unexpected possibilities… whilst also suggesting an impulsive edge that could lead you to jump first and think later… so be sure to take advantage of any sudden windows of opportunity but be mindful to reflect before launching full speed ahead.

 The Balsamic Moon or Waning Crescent Moon – from 5 September to 10 September passing through Gemini, Cancer, Leo, and into Virgo

Right at the start of this phase, as the Moon moves from Gemini into Cancer the energy indicates the potential for issues of inequality or unfairness to be brought to the fore, and these issues may well surface within personal relationships as well as on the global stage. This focus then sets the energetic pace for the entire period, with the higher purpose calling you to focus your attention on what you can personally do to bring about positive changes in any areas affected by these kinds of dynamics and to generate healing. Each time the Moon passes from one sign to another this energetic is intensified, so be mindful of these pockets in time and engage your reflective practise before taking considered actions grounded in emotional awareness of the potential consequences and outcomes.

The New Moon – 11 September – 18°25' Virgo

The flavour of inequality and unfairness of the previous Moon time continues… but although there is an underlying energetic of unrest in the larger astrodynamics today, this is accompanied by some strongly positive collaborations that suggest rebirth and healing through a connection with higher and spiritual values.
And so whatever is happening in the context of your personal world… or in a more global context, the influence of this New Moon presents the perfect opportunity to set wishes and intentions that focus your attention on what you can actually do in real and practical ways to move your manifestations forwards, especially in any areas where you are seeking resolutions and healing… both internally and externally… and if you suffer from any form of self-doubt or a raging inner critic, the energy of this Moon will assist in moving beyond these limiting beliefs.

New Moon Global Timings:
Los Angeles, USA   Thu, 10 Sep 2026 at 20:26 PDT
New York, USA   Thu, 10 Sep 2026 at 23:26 EDT
Reykjavik, Iceland   Fri, 11 Sep 2026 at 03:26 GMT
London, UK   Fri, 11 Sep 2026 at 04:26 BST
Paris, France   Fri, 11 Sep 2026 at 05:26 CEST
Cape Town, SA   Fri, 11 Sep 2026 at 05:26 SAST
Delhi, India   Fri, 11 Sep 2026 at 08:56 IST
Perth, Australia   Fri, 11 Sep 2026 at 11:26 AWST
Tokyo, Japan   Fri, 11 Sep 2026 at 12:26 JST
Sydney, Australia   Fri, 11 Sep 2026 at 13:26 AEST
Auckland, NZ   Fri, 11 Sep 2026 at 15:26 NZST
GMT/UTC   Fri, 11 Sep 2026 at 03:26 GMT

 The Waxing Crescent Moon – from 12 September to 17 September – passing through Libra, Scorpio, and Sagittarius

This Moon time begins with a burst of activity and although the overall planetary collaborations are very auspicious, the astro-dynamics also indicate the potential for some confusion and/or a lack of clarity… so if you experience any uncertainty, be sure to realign and bring yourself back into balance before moving anything forwards.
As this Moon phase progresses, the overall flavour is very up and down, creating a bit of a roller coaster kind of energetic with an emphasis on communication, suggesting that it will pay you to identify what sits beneath the surface as well as what is immediately being stated… whether this is you in communication with yourself… or in your communications with others.

The First Quarter Moon – 18 September – 25°57' Sagittarius

This First Quarter Moon invites you to expand your perceptions and horizons and to embrace solutions and outcomes that contribute to a world of fairness and equality… and the overall astro-dynamics today place a powerful emphasis on personal and realistic review. So if you are actively engaged in restructuring your circumstances or the quality of your relationships this Moon time will feel very supportive… however, even if events arrive that initiate unexpected changes, then the overall flavour of the day will help you to get still and through mindful reflection, create open, realistic conversations that find beneficial solutions.

The Waxing Gibbous Moon – from 19 September to 25 September passing through Capricorn, Aquarius, and Pisces

For most of this Moon phase the energy flows reasonably well with a great emphasis on real and practical actions that create healing… and whilst there are some undercurrents of tension the overall flow of positivity far outweighs any discord! Fab… however, at the latter end of this period when the Moon moves into and through Pisces there is a distinct shift that brings a far more intense energetic… and even there are strong surges of positivity that strongly support rebirth and evolution, there are also some highly emotionally charged undertones that suggest defensiveness… or the potential for buttons to be pressed… or even the revisiting or resurfacing of old wounds… so if any vulnerabilities surface in either yourself or others, try to respond with empathy and sensitivity.

The Full Moon – 26 September – 03°37' Aries

The energetics of this Full Moon are a fascinating mix! On the one hand there are some seriously powerful energies that suggest potential tension… confusion… feelings of unfairness… and with old wounds being brought to the surface… on the other hand, there are equally strong powerfully positive dynamics that generate transformation through higher minded solutions and out-of-the-box thinking! A Full Moon naturally illuminates what we need to see so we can then make informed choices that support conscious actions… and the energy of Aries brings a very personal focus to the essence of the day… so perhaps we should each ask ourselves what we want to do with this energy… get still… notice… listen… and observe… and then make very conscious choices that align our actions with everything that we want to see in the world!

Full Moon Global Timings:
Los Angeles, USA	Sat, 26 Sep 2026 at 09:48 PDT
New York, USA	Sat, 26 Sep 2026 at 12:48 EDT
Reykjavik, Iceland	Sat, 26 Sep 2026 at 16:48 GMT
London, UK	Sat, 26 Sep 2026 at 17:48 BST
Paris, France	Sat, 26 Sep 2026 at 18:48 CEST
Cape Town, SA	Sat, 26 Sep 2026 at 18:48 SAST
Delhi, India	Sat, 26 Sep 2026 at 22:18 IST
Perth, Australia	Sun, 27 Sep 2026 at 00:48 AWST
Tokyo, Japan	Sun, 27 Sep 2026 at 01:48 JST
Sydney, Australia	Sun, 27 Sep 2026 at 02:48 AEST
Auckland, NZ	Sun, 27 Sep 2026 at 05:48 NZDT
GMT/UTC	Sat, 26 Sep 2026 at 16:48 GMT

The Disseminating or Waning Gibbous Moon – from 27 September to 2 October passing through Aries, Taurus, Gemini, and into Cancer

This Moon phase feels immensely significant simply because of the strength and power of the overall dynamics! Although the Lunar energy is gently diminishing during this period, the planetary connections are heating up and building in significant intensity! Curiously, underneath the surface some extremely auspicious collaborations remain throughout which is fabulous and holds a wonderful space of possibility... however, I have a concern that this potential could be overshadowed by the intensity of the other more discordant energies. The key to success lies in your personal awareness of the energy and your ability to be responsive... rather than re-active... so this Moon time is a good test of self-mastery!

August / September 2026

31 Monday
Aries • VOC (12h 15m)

Waning Gibbous Moon
Late Summer Bank Holiday - UK

---

1 Tuesday
VOC • Taurus

Waning Gibbous Moon

---

2 Wednesday
Taurus • VOC (25h 1m)

Waning Gibbous Moon

---

3 Thursday
VOC • Gemini

Waning Gibbous Moon Phase ends

---

4 Friday
Gemini

Last Quarter Moon 11°48' Gemini

September 2026

Journalling and Notes

5 **Saturday**
Gemini • VOC (5h 52m) • Cancer

Waning Crescent Moon Phase starts

6 **Sunday**
Cancer

Waning Crescent Moon
Father's Day - Australia & New Zealand

September 2026

7   Monday

Cancer • VOC (3h 11m) • Leo

Waning Crescent Moon
Labor Day – USA

8   Tuesday

Leo

Waning Crescent Moon

9   Wednesday

Leo • VOC (38m) • Virgo

Waning Crescent Moon

10   Thursday

Virgo

Waning Crescent Moon Phase ends
Venus Enters Scorpio, Mercury Enters Libra, Uranus Retrograde Begins

11   Friday

Virgo • VOC (18h 1m)

New Moon 18°25' Virgo

September 2026

Journalling and Notes

12 Saturday
VOC • Libra

Waxing Crescent Moon Phase starts

13 Sunday
Libra • VOC (16h 18m)

Waxing Crescent Moon

September 2026

---

14 Monday

VOC • Scorpio

Waxing Crescent Moon
Lilith Enters Capricorn

---

15 Tuesday

Scorpio

Waxing Crescent Moon

---

16 Wednesday

Scorpio • VOC (13h 12m) • Sagittarius

Waxing Crescent Moon

---

17 Thursday

Sagittarius

Waxing Crescent Moon Phase ends

---

18 Friday

Sagittarius • VOC (8h 12m)

First Quarter Moon 25°57' Sagittarius
Chiron (Retrograde) Leaves Taurus

September 2026

Journalling and Notes

---

19 Saturday

VOC • Capricorn

Waxing Gibbous Moon Phase starts

---

20 Sunday

Capricorn

Waxing Gibbous Moon

September 2026

21 Monday
Capricorn • VOC (2h 44m) • Aquarius

Waxing Gibbous Moon

22 Tuesday
Aquarius

Waxing Gibbous Moon

23 Wednesday
Aquarius • VOC (19h 6m)

Waxing Gibbous Moon
Sun Enters Libra
Autumn Equinox Northern Hemisphere – Spring Equinox Southern Hemisphere

24 Thursday
VOC • Pisces

Waxing Gibbous Moon

25 Friday
Pisces

Waxing Gibbous Moon Phase ends

September 2026

Journalling and Notes

26 Saturday

Pisces • VOC (1h 52m) • Aries

Full Moon 03°37' Aries

27 Sunday

Aries

Waning Gibbous Moon Phase starts
New Zealand Clocks Change

Desires, Goals and Intentions for October 2026

Welcome to October 2026

October 2026... Get Still... Remain Grounded... And Reflect and Review

October is not without intensity... and right at the start of the month we see some of the most powerful and potentially discordant planetary dynamics of the entire year... however, the Full Moon marks a significant shift in the energy and even though some strong dynamics continue throughout the month, we also see other dynamics and planetary collaborations that bring a flavour of massive creative potential. Relationships are also brought into focus and whether this is your relationship with yourself... or your relationship with the divine and your higher self... or your relationships in general... family, friends, partners and lovers... the energetics offer an opportunity to really assess and evaluate... and at depth!

The key to navigating the more turbulent energetics is to remain grounded at all times... and steady in your actions... while simultaneously being open to whatever you are shown...

Our first card of Authenticity urges you to remain true to your highest values and assisting in all aspects of healthy relationships... to shed any masks that you have previously felt you had to wear... aligning with Perth the Rune of Initiation, this collaboration remind us that your Spiritual awakening is a deeply personal experience and not everyone will growing at the same pace as you... So observe and be true to yourself and the highest and best version of you!

Our second card of Don't Wobble reinforces the need to get still... review and evaluate... before taking action! With so much retrograde energy present during this month there will inevitably be some delays or interruptions or simply some slowing down... but with purpose! A human life is not designed to move full speed ahead, every day, all of the time... and pockets of slower energy create opportunity for review and evaluation and indeed to revisit areas that need realigning to ensure that future growth can flourish. This card aligns with Kano, the Rune of Openings, acknowledging that even when the world appears to be somewhat disruptive, new directions are being forged... so hold the positive... hold the higher perspective... when needed hold your ground... and remain anchored and on a daily basis be responsive rather than reactive!

Cards and Runes October 2026

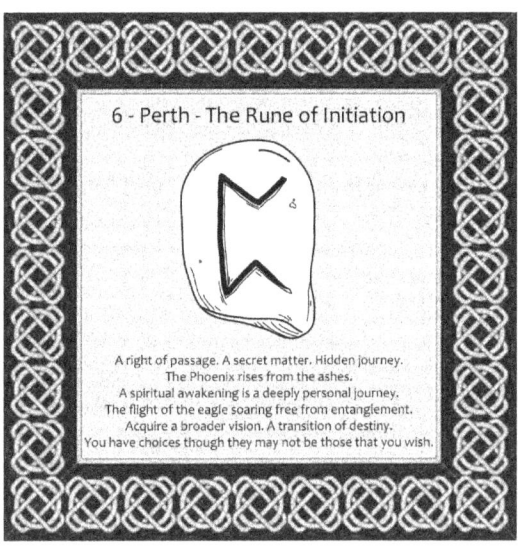

Cards and Runes October 2026

Don't Wobble
13

Are you having a wobble?
Whether a minor one or a Major one this is completely understandable... you are facing tough choices... but deep inside yourself you know what you need to do! This card is here to validate your deeper knowing and the decisions that you are making. As you move forwards, your anxiety will ease and you will refind your balance.

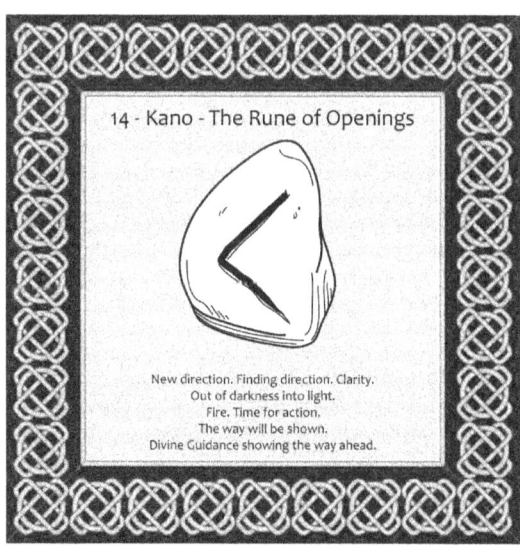

14 - Kano - The Rune of Openings

New direction. Finding direction. Clarity.
Out of darkness into light.
Fire. Time for action.
The way will be shown.
Divine Guidance showing the way ahead.

Moon Phases October 2026

 The Disseminating or Waning Gibbous Moon – from 27 September to 2 October passing through Aries, Taurus, Gemini, and into Cancer

This Moon phase feels immensely significant simply because of the strength and power of the overall dynamics! Although the Lunar energy is gently diminishing during this period, the planetary connections are heating up and building in significant intensity! Curiously, underneath the surface some extremely auspicious collaborations remain throughout which is fabulous and holds a wonderful space of possibility... however, I have a concern that this potential could be overshadowed by the intensity of the other more discordant energies. The key to success lies in your personal awareness of the energy and your ability to be responsive... rather than re-active... so this Moon time is a good test of self-mastery!

 The Last Quarter Moon – 3 October – 10°21' Cancer

When I write this diary my intention is to give you a genuine flavour of the overall energy and even if there are discordant energies, to highlight the higher energetic in every situation and the positive potential within those energies. Today the energy is intense... to put it mildly and whilst the overall dynamics today suggest an opportunity for evaluation, this may arise due to a build-up of tension or a culmination of events, or because hidden agendas become apparent with issues brought to the surface that can no longer be avoided... and these energetics could create intense communications with the potential for power struggles and even confrontation! The key as always is to remain anchored and grounded... and remember... awareness creates empowerment and conscious personal choice!

 The Balsamic Moon or Waning Crescent Moon – from 4 October to 9 October passing through Cancer, Leo, Virgo, and into Libra

For the first couple of days of this Moon time the intensity of the Quarter Moon continues. The higher vibration of these dynamics brings an energy of creativity, passion, and guidance through spiritual awakening... but given the strength of the discordant energies the circumstances that drive these positive transformations may not arrive with ease. The energy then flows more readily... yea... suggesting opportunities for positive expansion and progression... and with an added flavour of karmic divine timing! Just before the New Moon the energy intensifies again, however there is a beautifully reflective energetic present, so if circumstances arrive that slow you down, then trust there is purpose to this and reflect on any interruptions with grace!

The New Moon – 10 October – 17°21' Libra

Today our beautiful Moon joins the Sun in harmonious balanced Libra… so whatever has taken place in the intensity of the previous two Moon phases this is a perfect day to commit to realigning and rebalancing your own personal energetic field… and also to review your own goals to ensure they are in harmony with everything you wish to create in your world.
There is an undertone of depth in the overall planetary collaborations that could bring profound insights and deep internal awareness particularly in areas of relationship… so let love be your guide… and if at all possible, create time today to meditate or simply just to slow down and reflect.

New Moon Global Timings:
Los Angeles, USA	Sat, 10 Oct 2026 at 08:49 PDT
New York, USA	Sat, 10 Oct 2026 at 11:49 EDT
Reykjavik, Iceland	Sat, 10 Oct 2026 at 15:49 GMT
London, UK	Sat, 10 Oct 2026 at 16:49 BST
Paris, France	Sat, 10 Oct 2026 at 17:49 CEST
Cape Town, SA	Sat, 10 Oct 2026 at 17:49 SAST
Delhi, India	Sat, 10 Oct 2026 at 21:19 IST
Perth, Australia	Sat, 10 Oct 2026 at 23:49 AWST
Tokyo, Japan	Sun, 11 Oct 2026 at 00:49 JST
Sydney, Australia	Sun, 11 Oct 2026 at 02:49 AEDT
Auckland, NZ	Sun, 11 Oct 2026 at 04:49 NZDT
GMT/UTC	Sat, 10 Oct 2026 at 15:49 GMT

 The Waxing Crescent Moon – from 11 October to 17 October passing through Libra, Scorpio, Sagittarius, and Capricorn

This Moon phase can be divided into two very distinct stages…

An intense start brings a push-pull energetic suggesting desires to move forwards and yet also potential uncertainty about how to actually do this… and this may well involve revisiting insecurities that contribute to a lack of confidence but are no longer relevant to you… healing is needed… however…

When the Moon reaches Sagittarius there is a huge shift in the energy bringing a wonderfully positive flow that also combines with a dynamic that can indicate sudden and even unexpected opportunities that are simultaneously also very grounded… fab!

Right at the end of this Moon time the Lunar energy intensifies again… but this is brief!

The First Quarter Moon – 18 October – 25°18' Capricorn (see VOC Moons p.212)

The exact time of this First Quarter Moon begins a nine hour Void of Course period. Depending on your unique personal circumstances this could feel extremely liberating or a bit fast paced and all over the place! The overall dynamics today place an emphasis on relationships, and whether this is some aspect of your relationship with yourself… or with the divine and your higher self… or your relationships in general… family, friends, partners, and lovers… today the energy invites review and may well highlight areas of relationship that call for your attention to enable healthy growth and progression and if needed, completion and/or resolution through healing.

 The Waxing Gibbous Moon – from 19 October to 25 October passing through Aquarius, Pisces, Aries, and into Taurus

The first half of this Moon time brings some strong spikes of energy… and on a regular basis! If events in your world are going well then these surges could really enhance your progress… yea… but if events in your world are moving faster than you would like this could feel a bit disruptive… so remember in between the more intense surges there are pockets of greater steadiness… so be observant and take time to breathe whenever the energy accommodates this. The Moon also links with a powerful karmic energetic and so whatever is happening in your world there will be a higher purpose to any disruption. The day before the Full Moon the energy intensifies significantly and holds in strength so if fast-paced change is currently a challenge for you be aware of this and prepare your schedule accordingly ahead of time!

 The Super Full Moon – 26 October – 02°45' Taurus

The energetics of this Moon suggest the unearthing or revealing of hidden depths particularly within relationships… suggesting that through open and honest communication, powerful collaborations of profound depth could be forged… however, if any challenges within your relationships, either with yourself or with others, have not really been previously adequately processed, this Moon may well reveal these areas of tension… but this is with purpose! The overall astro-dynamics today are actively promoting transformation through emotional and spiritual awareness with our beautiful Moon offering you the potential to receive significant illuminations and guidance that can then be applied to bring about gentle progression and where needed, healing and release.

Full Moon Global Timings:

Los Angeles, USA	Sun, 25 Oct 2026 at 21:11 PDT
New York, USA	Mon, 26 Oct 2026 at 00:11 EDT
Reykjavik, Iceland	Mon, 26 Oct 2026 at 04:11 GMT
London, UK	Mon, 26 Oct 2026 at 04:11 GMT
Paris, France	Mon, 26 Oct 2026 at 05:11 CET
Cape Town, SA	Mon, 26 Oct 2026 at 06:11 SAST
Delhi, India	Mon, 26 Oct 2026 at 09:41 IST
Perth, Australia	Mon, 26 Oct 2026 at 12:11 AWST
Tokyo, Japan	Mon, 26 Oct 2026 at 13:11 JST
Sydney, Australia	Mon, 26 Oct 2026 at 15:11 AEDT
Auckland, NZ	Mon, 26 Oct 2026 at 17:11 NZDT
GMT/UTC	Mon, 26 Oct 2026 at 04:11 GMT

The Disseminating or Waning Gibbous Moon – from 27 October to 31 October passing through Taurus, Gemini, and Cancer

The overall flow of energy during this Moon time is a bit of a mixed bag… on the one hand the planetary collaborations suggest some areas of potential tension… on the other hand an underlying flow of more gentle energy prevails throughout… and with so many planets currently in retrograde, interruptions, and diversions, may well occur! This phase of the Moon naturally favours steady progress and so rather than viewing any delays with frustration, recognise that retrograde energy arrives with purpose… a human life is not designed to move full speed ahead, every day, all of the time. Pockets of slower energy create opportunity for review and evaluation and indeed to revisit areas that need realigning to ensure that future growth can flourish. So, try to use the mix of energy with awareness… and on a daily basis be responsive rather than reactive.

September / October 2026

28 Monday

Aries • VOC (4h 50m) • Taurus

Waning Gibbous Moon
Mars Enters Leo

---

29 Tuesday

Taurus

Waning Gibbous Moon

---

30 Wednesday

Taurus • VOC (17h 51m) • Gemini

Waning Gibbous Moon
Mercury Enters Scorpio

---

1 Thursday

Gemini

Waning Gibbous Moon
Don't forget to order your 2027 Manifest with the Moon Astro-Moon Diary!

---

2 Friday

Gemini • VOC (17h 13m) • Cancer

Waning Gibbous Moon Phase ends

October 2026

Journalling and Notes

3   Saturday
Cancer • VOC (31h 46m)

Last Quarter Moon 10°21' Cancer
Venus Retrograde Begins

4   Sunday
VOC

Waning Crescent Moon Phase starts
Australia Clocks Change

October 2026

---
5 Monday

VOC • Leo

Waning Crescent Moon

---
6 Tuesday

Leo • VOC (16h 32m)

Waning Crescent Moon

---
7 Wednesday

VOC • Virgo • VOC (37h 15m)

Waning Crescent Moon

---
8 Thursday

VOC

Waning Crescent Moon

---
9 Friday

VOC • Libra

Waning Crescent Moon Phase ends

October 2026

Journalling and Notes

---

10 Saturday

Libra

New Moon 17°21' Libra

---

11 Sunday

Libra • VOC (16h 14m) • Scorpio

Waxing Crescent Moon Phase starts

October 2026

12 Monday

Scorpio

Waxing Crescent Moon
Indigenous Peoples Day – USA

---

13 Tuesday

Scorpio • VOC (16h 15m)

Waxing Crescent Moon

---

14 Wednesday

VOC • Sagittarius

Waxing Crescent Moon

---

15 Thursday

Sagittarius • VOC (15h 2m)

Waxing Crescent Moon

---

16 Friday

VOC • Capricorn

Waxing Crescent Moon
Pluto Retrograde Ends

October 2026

Journalling and Notes

17 Saturday
Capricorn

Waxing Crescent Moon Phase ends

18 Sunday
Capricorn • VOC (9h 28m)

First Quarter Moon 25°18' Capricorn

October 2026

19 Monday
VOC • Aquarius

Waxing Gibbous Moon Phase starts

20 Tuesday
Aquarius

Waxing Gibbous Moon

21 Wednesday
Aquarius • VOC (3h 53m) • Pisces

Waxing Gibbous Moon

22 Thursday
Pisces

Waxing Gibbous Moon

23 Friday
Pisces • VOC (16h 24m) • Aries

Waxing Gibbous Moon
Sun Enters Scorpio

October 2026

Journalling and Notes

---

24 Saturday

Aries

Waxing Gibbous Moon
Mercury Retrograde Begins

---

25 Sunday

Aries

Waxing Gibbous Moon Phase ends
Venus (Retrograde) Leaves Scorpio
UK & Central Europe Clocks Change

October 2026

26 Monday
Aries • VOC (36m) • Taurus

Super Full Moon 02°45' Taurus

27 Tuesday
Taurus • VOC (10h 12m)

Waning Gibbous Moon Phase starts

28 Wednesday
VOC • Gemini

Waning Gibbous Moon

29 Thursday
Gemini • VOC (4h 23m)

Waning Gibbous Moon

30 Friday
VOC • Cancer

Waning Gibbous Moon

October / November 2026

Journalling and Notes

31 **Saturday**
Cancer • VOC (6h 19m)

Waning Gibbous Moon Phase ends
Festivals of Samhain Northern Hemisphere – Beltane Southern Hemisphere
Have you ordered your 2027 Manifest with the Moon Astro-Moon Diary?

1 **Sunday**
VOC • Leo

Last Quarter Moon 09°25' Leo
USA & Canada Clocks Change

Desires, Goals and Intentions for November 2026

Welcome to November 2026

November 2026… Fast Paced Change and Transformation… The Universe is in Charge!

November is a month when the astro-dynamics both flows freely… and yet may also present us with challenges. Throughout the month a consistent and positive flow of energy constantly supports… indeed pushes, for transformation and change… and there are also some big planetary alignments that bring a karmic energy suggesting synchronistic events and divine timing to aid and expand transformation and change… whether we like it or not! Further underlying dynamics also suggest that we may be called to revisit issues from the past that have remained unresolved and that through reflection and retrospective thinking we can find better ways to deal with conflicts and problems and mistakes and move forwards with higher minded solutions that honour new ways of thinking, being, and doing!

Our first card of Imperfection acknowledges the value of mistakes… providing they are openly owned and used as a tool for evaluation and healthy healing. Aligning with Fehu, the Rune of Possessions, this combination suggests that part of the evaluation and review needed may well involve the distribution of commodities and the need for success to be underpinned by humility.

Our second card of The Spiritual Warrior makes a bold statement and also serves as an invitation that asks us each to align with the calling of the Universe and to navigate these changing times with a heightened awareness of a much bigger picture! Collaborating with Hagalaz, the Rune of Disruption, who is also sometimes known as 'The Great Awakener'… this combination acknowledges and validates that we are spiritual beings navigating a human journey and that right now through disruption, we are awakening… and that both individually and collectively, humanity is being called to step up… so that realistic, higher minded solutions can be found to resolve the challenges that humanity has created and now faces…

This is a powerful month, fast-paced and happening… loaded with opportunity through profound restructuring, and the Universe is backing all who are striving to heal and align with higher minded solutions… so step into the best version of you and lean into the change.

Cards and Runes November 2026

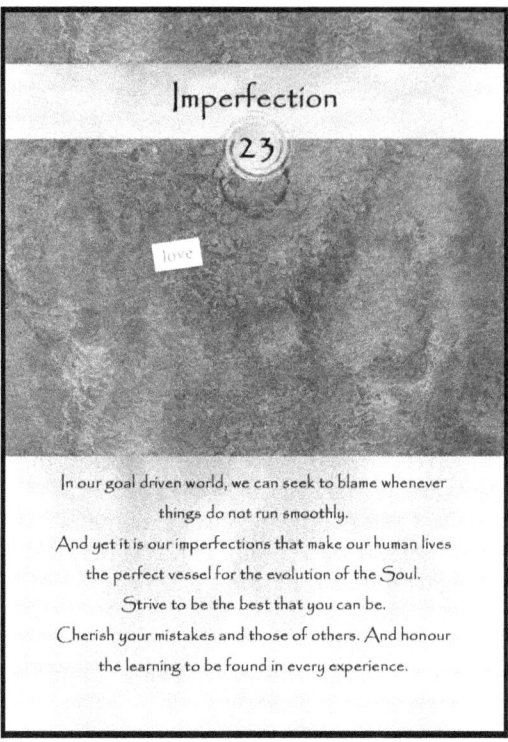

In our goal driven world, we can seek to blame whenever things do not run smoothly.
And yet it is our imperfections that make our human lives the perfect vessel for the evolution of the Soul.
Strive to be the best that you can be.
Cherish your mistakes and those of others. And honour the learning to be found in every experience.

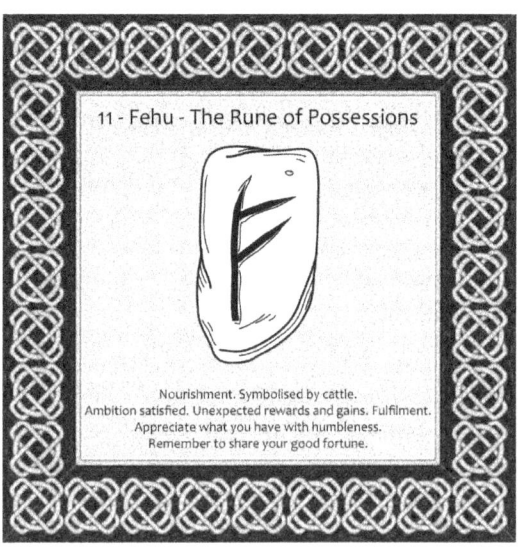

Nourishment. Symbolised by cattle.
Ambition satisfied. Unexpected rewards and gains. Fulfilment.
Appreciate what you have with humbleness.
Remember to share your good fortune.

Cards and Runes November 2026

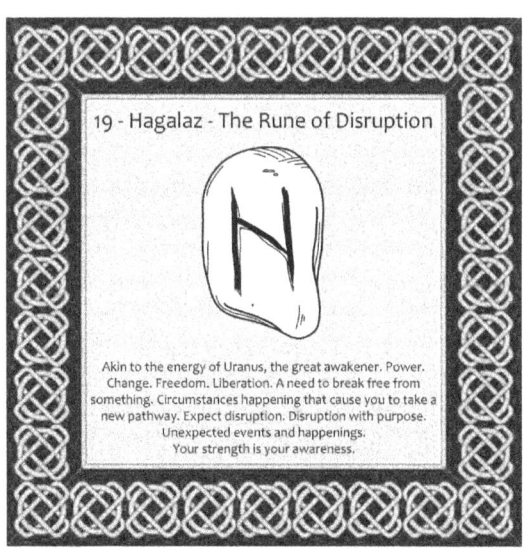

Moon Phases November 2026

 The Last Quarter Moon – 1 November – 09°25′ Leo

Today the astro-dynamics offer a fabulous opportunity for a personal check-in. Aligning with the energy of the Earth festivals of Samhain in the Northern Hemisphere and Beltane in the Southern Hemisphere, this is a perfect day to validate and acknowledge where you are right now and all of your achievements in all areas of your life before moving into the next cycle of the Earths Calender. We are currently navigating a period of extraordinary transformation for humanity at large and in our personal circumstances and on both the global stage this can frequently involve monumental upheaval... so use the energy today for constructive, positive, self-reflection... the energy today supports realistic appraisal with constructive valuable feedback that emphasises the positive whilst acknowledging the enormity of the changes that are affecting us all!

 The Balsamic Moon or Waning Crescent Moon – from 2 November to 8 November passing through Leo, Virgo, Libra, and Scorpio

Following the delightful energetics of positive review that were so supported by the planetary alignments at the Last Quarter Moon, this period holds the positivity and gets off to a flying start with divine timing indicated, bringing movement and positive progression. The Lunar energy then favours consistent steady movement, nothing too fast, but also with the promise of potential openings and synchronistic windows of opportunity showing up... and potentially unexpectedly. This dynamic continues and even though there are some stronger spikes of astro-energy from time to time, this is more likely to support you... or indeed nudge you forwards, than bring any major hindrances.

 The New Moon – 9 November – 16°53′ Scorpio

The overall dynamics of today's New Moon highlights two complementary areas of focus, both of which support a powerfully positive flow of energy that actively promotes expansion, through balance and healing and in real practical ways. Firstly relationships are favourably indicated with planetary alignments that suggest the potential to expand your connections and move your relationships to a whole new level of depth and meaning... and secondly, communications are favoured suggesting the ability to smooth out difficulties and heal any differences. Tuning in with the depth of the Scorpio energy, any wishes and intentions set today will harness these dynamics and enhance new depths of genuine understanding.

New Moon Global Timings:
Los Angeles, USA	Sun, 8 Nov 2026 at 23:01 PST
New York, USA	Mon, 9 Nov 2026 at 02:01 EST
Reykjavik, Iceland	Mon, 9 Nov 2026 at 07:01 GMT
London, UK	Mon, 9 Nov 2026 at 07:01 GMT
Paris, France	Mon, 9 Nov 2026 at 08:01 CET
Cape Town, SA	Mon, 9 Nov 2026 at 09:01 SAST
Delhi, India	Mon, 9 Nov 2026 at 12:31 IST
Perth, Australia	Mon, 9 Nov 2026 at 15:01 AWST
Tokyo, Japan	Mon, 9 Nov 2026 at 16:01 JST
Sydney, Australia	Mon, 9 Nov 2026 at 18:01 AEDT
Auckland, NZ	Mon, 9 Nov 2026 at 20:01 NZDT
GMT/UTC	Mon, 9 Nov 2026 at 07:01 GMT

The Waxing Crescent Moon – from 10 November to 16 November passing through Sagittarius, Capricorn, and Aquarius

The overall flow of Lunar energy throughout this Moon phase is largely positive, upbeat, and supporting a forward motion that gathers with steady momentum… so whatever is taking place in your personal world, seize the moment and get going!
As the Moon navigates through each sign she touches base with some other more intense energies, however these pockets of Lunar intensity are relatively fleeting and are far more likely to bring events and circumstances to help you to stay on track with greater clarity and a clearer focus… so if anything appears to stop your progress, pay attention… it may be that adjustment is needed.

The First Quarter Moon – 17 November – 25°08' Aquarius

The dynamics of this Moon directly connect with an energy of karmic fate and destiny… and given that a First Quarter Moon is often associated with external events and circumstances that call you to review and evaluate, it will be fascinating to see what emerges for us each on this day.

The karmic alignments suggest that something could come to a head or arrive in a manner that is pushing for change and expansion, and yet the intensity of these influences are beautifully balanced by an underlying energetic of positive planetary alignments that suggest opportunities and solutions flowing with ease…

And so if any form of challenge lands in your world today, it will almost certainly be accompanied by an accessible solution.

The Waxing Gibbous Moon – from 18 November to 23 November passing through Pisces, Aries, and Taurus

During this Moon phase the overall astrodynamics bring an abundance of positive alignments, but with an underlying very fast-paced energy of expansion and flow… and rather like a river in full motion… it would be pretty difficult to stop the energy from moving forwards… however there is also a very strong dynamic that can indicate the potential for some more challenging circumstances to arrive… so if your world is expanding and overflowing with positivity this period will feel fabulous… everything is happening… and fast… however if more challenging circumstances are present in your world and you'd like to just slow things down, then you could experience frustration. There is also an additional undertone of fate and destiny present… so whatever is taking place, fasten your seatbelt and trust that that the Universe is in charge!

 The Super Full Moon – 24 November – 02°20' Gemini

This Super Full Moon in Gemini aligns with Uranus whose energy is sometimes referred to as the Great Awakener, bringing unexpected and sudden events and circumstances… but also higher-minded solutions and out-of-the-box thinking! And because a Super Moon is very close to the Earth the energy today is turbocharged! Now add additional planetary alignments that are not only calling for change but also forging ahead and pushing for expansion… and so the dynamics today could well indicate an intense time… however, the role of our beautiful Moon at her fullest is to illuminate and bring to light all that must be seen to generate much needed awakening and much needed changes… so lean into the higher vibration of possibility and out-of-the-box solutions and expect the unexpected!

Full Moon Global Timings:
Los Angeles, USA   Tue, 24 Nov 2026 at 06:53 PST
New York, USA   Tue, 24 Nov 2026 at 09:53 EST
Reykjavik, Iceland   Tue, 24 Nov 2026 at 14:53 GMT
London, UK   Tue, 24 Nov 2026 at 14:53 GMT
Paris, France   Tue, 24 Nov 2026 at 15:53 CET
Cape Town, SA   Tue, 24 Nov 2026 at 16:53 SAST
Delhi, India   Tue, 24 Nov 2026 at 20:23 IST
Perth, Australia   Tue, 24 Nov 2026 at 22:53 AWST
Tokyo, Japan   Tue, 24 Nov 2026 at 23:53 JST
Sydney, Australia   Wed, 25 Nov 2026 at 01:53 AEDT
Auckland, NZ   Wed, 25 Nov 2026 at 03:53 NZDT
GMT/UTC   Tue, 24 Nov 2026 at 14:53 GMT

The Disseminating or Waning Gibbous Moon – from 25 November to 30 November passing through Gemini, Cancer, Leo, and into Virgo

The theme of ongoing change and transformation continues, it is as though the Universe is demanding restructure in any and all ways of thinking, being, and doing, that no longer serve, both individually and as a collective… and during this time, we may well find ourselves revisiting previous issues that have yet to be resolved. As our beautiful Moon journeys through Cancer emotionality may intensify, however reflective retrospective thinking will assist in any areas of much needed growth. This is a time of profound restructuring, and the Universe is backing all who are striving to heal and align with higher minded solutions… so step into the best version of you and lean into the change.

November 2026

---
2 Monday

Leo

Waning Crescent Moon Phase starts

---
3 Tuesday

Leo • VOC (8h 18m) • Virgo

Waning Crescent Moon

---
4 Wednesday

Virgo • VOC (31h 41m)

Waning Crescent Moon

---
5 Thursday

VOC • Libra

Waning Crescent Moon

---
6 Friday

Libra

Waning Crescent Moon

November 2026

Journalling and Notes

---

7 Saturday
Libra • VOC (9h 21m)

Waning Crescent Moon

---

8 Sunday
VOC • Scorpio

Waning Crescent Moon Phase ends
Remembrance Sunday – UK

November 2026

9 Monday
Scorpio

New Moon 16°53' Scorpio

10 Tuesday
Scorpio • VOC (9h 12m) • Sagittarius

Waxing Crescent Moon Phase starts

11 Wednesday
Sagittarius

Waxing Crescent Moon
Veterans Day – USA

12 Thursday
Sagittarius • VOC (8h 59m) • Capricorn

Waxing Crescent Moon

13 Friday
Capricorn

Waxing Crescent Moon
Mercury Retrograde Ends

November 2026

Journalling and Notes

---

14 Saturday
Capricorn • VOC (14h 29m)

Waxing Crescent Moon
Venus Retrograde Ends

---

15 Sunday
VOC • Aquarius

Waxing Crescent Moon

November 2026

16 Monday
Aquarius

Waxing Crescent Moon Phase ends

17 Tuesday
Aquarius • VOC (6h 55m) • Pisces

First Quarter Moon 25°08' Aquarius

18 Wednesday
Pisces

Waxing Gibbous Moon Phase starts

19 Thursday
Pisces

Waxing Gibbous Moon

20 Friday
Pisces • VOC (4h 7m) • Aries

Waxing Gibbous Moon

November 2026

Journalling and Notes

---

21 Saturday

Aries

Waxing Gibbous Moon

---

22 Sunday

Aries • VOC (2h 32m) • Taurus

Waxing Gibbous Moon
Sun Enters Sagittarius

November 2026

23 Monday
Taurus

Waxing Gibbous Moon Phase ends

24 Tuesday
Taurus • VOC (1h 2m) • Gemini

Super Full Moon 02°20' Gemini

25 Wednesday
Gemini

Waning Gibbous Moon Phase starts

26 Thursday
Gemini • VOC (5h 28m) • Cancer

Waning Gibbous Moon
Mars Enters Virgo
Thanksgiving Day – USA

27 Friday
Cancer

Waning Gibbous Moon

November 2026

Journalling and Notes

28 Saturday
Cancer • VOC (5h 42m) • Leo

Waning Gibbous Moon

29 Sunday
Leo

Waning Gibbous Moon

Desires, Goals and Intentions for December 2026

Welcome to December 2026

December 2026... Stepping into the New... Destiny Unfolds!

December brings a mixed bag of energy... and this is not without tension... and yet within the powerful and often intense planetary collaborations this month there is huge potential to move beyond outdated ways, attitudes, structures, systems, and beliefs that no longer serve us, and step up and build new more resilient and sustainable ways of thinking, being, and doing, both individually and as a collective.

A powerful planetary alignment suggests that expansion will happen regardless... and with divine timing... it is as though Destiny is in charge, and the Universe is calling the shots... and our cards of Ground Yourself and Shine aligning with Isa the Rune of Standstill and Jeera the Rune of Harvest bring a powerful collective message!

At times of unprecedented acerated transformation, whether personally or globally, upheaval is inevitable... and the card of Ground Yourself reminds you to do exactly this... whatever is taking place, remain grounded... if at all possible go outside and if you can't then simply imagine yourself outdoors and connected with nature... and anchor yourself. This card sits with the energy and messages of Isa... which sometimes asks you to literally... Stand Still!

Stop... slow down... get grounded... recognise that you cannot always surge ahead... patience is needed with time to reflect and evaluate... and then... when the timing is right you will proceed...

Our second card of Shine then invites you to step up and be the very best and most amazing version of you, acknowledging the profound potential that is available for us each at this moment in time. Aligning with Jeera, this is a Rune of promise and of beneficial outcomes. This Rune is here to encourage you... now is the time to sow seeds that will create a sustainable future for generations yet to come and you have a part to play in this extraordinary transformation.

Cards and Runes December 2026

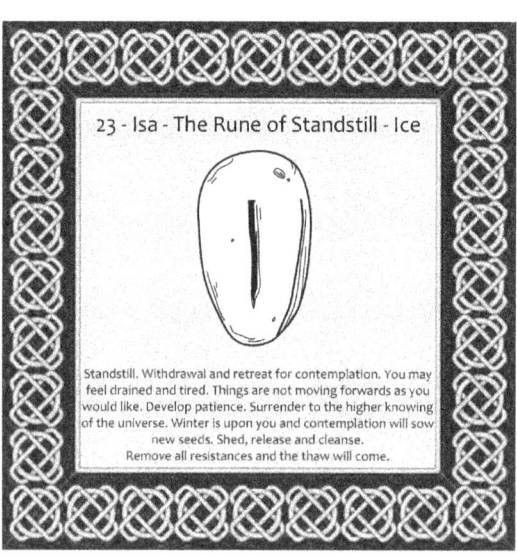

Cards and Runes December 2026

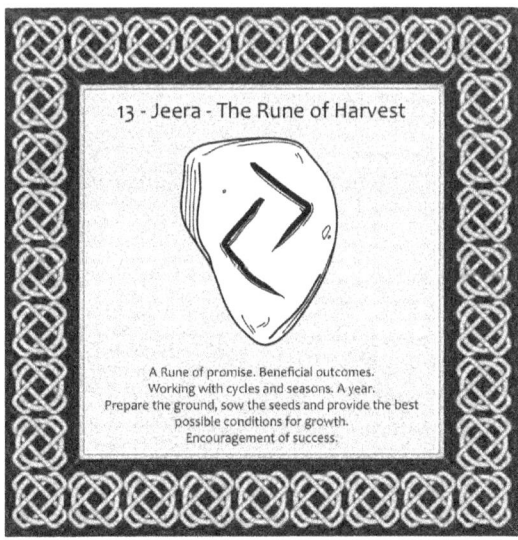

Moon Phases December 2026

 The Last Quarter Moon – 1 December – 09°03' Virgo

The dynamics of today's Moon bring a delightfully optimistic energetic to the current underlying planetary theme of karmic expansion... it is as though destiny herself is currently taking charge of accelerating the pace of change and transformation. A Last Quarter Moon naturally invites introspection and progression through reflection and internal evaluation... and the essence and energy of Virgo makes this a perfect day to get still and ask to receive clear pragmatic advice and guidance on what steps you can personally take to jump on board the fast-tracked energy of expansion... and if you are someone who is held back by a raging inner critic, ask for guidance to move through and beyond this limiting inner state of mind.

 The Balsamic Moon or Waning Crescent Moon – from 2 December to 8 December passing through Virgo, Libra, Scorpio, and Sagittarius

The energy of karmic expansion continues and even though the Lunar influence is diminishing the overall astro-dynamics heat up and as the Moon passes through Libra the energy is very up and down with a strong undertone of potential volatility with a need to break free from restriction. Whilst this could be acted out in a negative or lower vibrational way, the very same energetic creates openings for bold actions and breakthrough moments and profound personal empowerment! When the Moon then passes through Scorpio the overall flow of energy eases to a more flowing and steadier pace... however when the Moon moves into Sagittarius the intensity heats up yet again! So whatever is taking place in your world, consider your response... you have a choice!

 The New Moon – 9 December – 16°56' Sagittarius

The energetics of this New Moon are intense and tap into the underlying volatility and passionate desire for transformation and freedom from restriction... there is also an additional dynamic that can sometimes indicate power struggles particularly within relationships! However... this beautiful Moon sits in positive optimistic Sagittarius and also connects with an equally powerful and positive flow of energy that suggests new beginnings and fresh opportunities born of honesty, integrity, and the highest good for all! If there was ever a day to set and manifest wishes and intentions that honour peace on Earth then today the dynamics are perfect to do so! I personally wish you peace and happiness in all areas of your life, and may your joy radiate into the world bringing peace and light to all.

New Moon Global Timings:
Los Angeles, USA	Tue, 8 Dec 2026 at 16:51 PST
New York, USA	Tue, 8 Dec 2026 at 19:51 EST
Reykjavik, Iceland	Wed, 9 Dec 2026 at 00:51 GMT
London, UK	Wed, 9 Dec 2026 at 00:51 GMT
Paris, France	Wed, 9 Dec 2026 at 01:51 CET
Cape Town, SA	Wed, 9 Dec 2026 at 02:51 SAST
Delhi, India	Wed, 9 Dec 2026 at 06:21 IST
Perth, Australia	Wed, 9 Dec 2026 at 08:51 AWST
Tokyo, Japan	Wed, 9 Dec 2026 at 09:51 JST
Sydney, Australia	Wed, 9 Dec 2026 at 11:51 AEDT
Auckland, NZ	Wed, 9 Dec 2026 at 13:51 NZDT
GMT/UTC	Wed, 9 Dec 2026 at 00:51 GMT

The Waxing Crescent Moon – from 10 December to 16 December passing through Capricorn, Aquarius, and Pisces (See VOC Moons p.212)

At the start of the Moon time, although the energetics are still intense, a powerful dynamic suggests that open and honest communications could create extremely positive results… yea! The energy then intensifies however there is actually a good balance between the flow of positive openings and any more discordant planetary collaborations… perhaps tension will leverage traction resulting in positive outcomes! As the Moon approaches Aquarius she enters a massive 45 hour Void of Course period…. and simultaneously the more challenging planetary dynamics also ease, suggesting a time of genuine and positive flow… this continues and even though our beautiful Moon generates some more intense spikes of energy they are relatively fleeting and should arrive with synchronicity and serve to push you along and in the right direction!

The First Quarter Moon – 17 December – 25°17' Pisces

The overall energetics today are relatively gentle and today, our beautiful Moon leans into the planetary collaborations that are dissolving old ways that no longer serve us, whilst bringing opportunity to restructure and build new and more resilient ways and sustainable ways of thinking, being, and doing, both individually and as a collective.

A First Quarter Moon can present events that highlight anything that needs to be worked through so we can move forwards with greater ease and flow… so lean into the energy and observe… today may bring an opportunity that supports you to create positive transformation and restructure in some aspect of your world.

The Waxing Gibbous Moon – from 18 December to 23 December passing through Aries, Taurus, Gemini, and into Cancer

Throughout this Moon time the planetary alignments hold an incredibly positive dynamic… and it is consistent throughout the entire period… and added to by the Moon's own gathering of momentum and building Lunar energy! Whatever is happening in your world, take advantage of this energy and harness the potential to make things happen and move things forwards! During this period as the Moon passes or engages with some of the key astrological players you may well find that certain areas of your world are highlighted or emphasised or intensified… but given the profound positivity of this dynamic, if at any time any discord or unease or tension surfaces, you should be able to move your situation forwards with ease.

 The Super Full Moon – 24 December – 02°13' Cancer

The energetics of this Super Full Moon are powerful, to put it mildly… and with two very different, almost opposing energies…

On the one hand, the incredibly positive and flowing collaborations of the previous Moon time remain strong…
On the other hand, an equally strong collaboration of potential tension is also present, suggesting strong emotions and the potential for more extreme feelings to surface.

A Full Moon naturally illuminates what we need to see, and the Cancer influence may well highlight issues that carry emotional weight.. so if this is the case then get still, notice and observe… then lean into the positive energies that are aligned with expansion, synchronicities, and divine timing… and actively promote healthy open communications and healing.

Full Moon Global Timings:
Los Angeles, USA	Wed, 23 Dec 2026 at 17:27 PST
New York, USA	Wed, 23 Dec 2026 at 20:27 EST
Reykjavik, Iceland	Thu, 24 Dec 2026 at 01:27 GMT
London, UK	Thu, 24 Dec 2026 at 01:27 GMT
Paris, France	Thu, 24 Dec 2026 at 02:27 CET
Cape Town, SA	Thu, 24 Dec 2026 at 03:27 SAST
Delhi, India	Thu, 24 Dec 2026 at 06:57 IST
Perth, Australia	Thu, 24 Dec 2026 at 09:27 AWST
Tokyo, Japan	Thu, 24 Dec 2026 at 10:27 JST
Sydney, Australia	Thu, 24 Dec 2026 at 12:27 AEDT
Auckland, NZ	Thu, 24 Dec 2026 at 14:27 NZDT
GMT/UTC	Thu, 24 Dec 2026 at 01:27 GMT

The Disseminating or Waning Gibbous Moon – from 25 December to 29 December passing through Cancer, Leo, and Virgo

The astro-dynamics of this Moon phase bring an interesting mix of strong and sometimes conflicting energies. Whilst these collaborations could suggest some confusion… or touch on insecurities… and the kinds of thoughts and emotions that we can inevitably feel at times of instability and fast-paced changes, there are an equal number of powerfully positive dynamics that suggest the healing of old wounds, and the potential for opportunities to arise and for circumstances to flow in your favour. However these energies are arriving in your world… and it may well be a mix of both… lean into the positivity and let yourself grow.

 The Last Quarter Moon – 30 December – 09°05' Libra

This is a day of strong energies… however, the Lunar influence creates a kite formation with the Moon at the base, and this is particularly auspicious! Given the strength and potential tension of the overall energetics today this is a major bonus! The planetary collaborations suggest the breaking down and dissolving of old systems and outdated thought patterns and perspectives to make way for major restructuring in any areas that do not uphold the higher values of truth, equality, fairness, and sustainability for all… and whilst this is not a new theme, today these energies are very present and in strength… so take time to pause and meditate into the energy of the kite formation with positive intent.

 The Disseminating or Waning Crescent Moon – from 31 December to 6 January passing through Libra, Scorpio, Sagittarius, and into Capricorn

As we cross the threshold of the New Year the intensity of the energy eases considerably… and we see less tension and more flow… yea! As the Moon passes through Scorpio and into Sagittarius, relationships are emphasised and with a fated or karmic quality… perhaps our understanding of one another may move to a higher or whole new level. The overall astro-dynamics of this Moon time bring an overall impetus of onwards and upwards movement… New Year… new attitudes… new perspectives… it's time to move on, and in a positive way. Welcome to 2027!

November / December 2026

30 Monday
Leo • VOC (4h 3m) • Virgo

Waning Gibbous Moon Phase ends

1 Tuesday
Virgo

Last Quarter Moon 09°03' Virgo

2 Wednesday
Virgo • VOC (10h 54m) • Libra

Waning Crescent Moon Phase starts

3 Thursday
Libra

Waning Crescent Moon

4 Friday
Libra

Waning Crescent Moon
Venus Enters Scorpio

December 2026

Journalling and Notes

5 **Saturday**
Libra • VOC (5h 55m) • Scorpio

Waning Crescent Moon

6 **Sunday**
Scorpio

Waning Crescent Moon
Mercury Enters Sagittarius

December 2026

---

7 Monday

Scorpio • VOC (6h 00m) • Sagittarius

Waning Crescent Moon

---

8 Tuesday

Sagittarius

Waning Crescent Moon Phase ends

---

9 Wednesday

Sagittarius • VOC (6h 4m)

New Moon 16°56' Sagittarius

---

10 Thursday

VOC • Capricorn • VOC (44h 54m)

Waxing Crescent Moon Phase starts

---

11 Friday

VOC

Waxing Crescent Moon
Saturn Retrograde Ends

December 2026

Journalling and Notes

---

12 Saturday
VOC • Aquarius

Waxing Crescent Moon

---

13 Sunday
Aquarius

Waxing Crescent Moon
Neptune Retrograde Ends, Jupiter Retrograde Begins

December 2026

14 Monday
Aquarius

Waxing Crescent Moon

15 Tuesday
Aquarius • VOC (5h 57m) • Pisces

Waxing Crescent Moon

16 Wednesday
Pisces

Waxing Crescent Moon Phase ends

17 Thursday
Pisces • VOC (8h 53m) • Aries

First Quarter Moon 25°17' Aries

18 Friday
Aries

Waxing Gibbous Moon Phase starts

December 2026

Journalling and Notes

19 Saturday
Aries • VOC (3h 51m) • Taurus

Waxing Gibbous Moon

20 Sunday
Taurus

Waxing Gibbous Moon

December 2026

21 Monday
Taurus • VOC (5h 2m)

Waxing Gibbous Moon
Sun Enters Capricorn
Winter Solstice Northern Hemisphere – Summer Solstice Southern Hemisphere

22 Tuesday
VOC • Gemini

Waxing Gibbous Moon

23 Wednesday
Gemini • VOC (4h 59m) • Cancer

Waxing Gibbous Moon Phase ends

24 Thursday
Cancer

Super Full Moon 02°13' Cancer
Christmas Eve

25 Friday
Cancer • VOC (21h 3m) • Leo

Waning Gibbous Moon Phase starts
Mercury Enters Capricorn
Christmas Day

December 2026

Journalling and Notes

26 Saturday

Leo

Waning Gibbous Moon
Boxing Day, St. Stephen's Day – Ireland

27 Sunday

Leo • VOC (5h 35m)

Waning Gibbous Moon

December 2026 / January 2027

---
28 Monday
VOC • Virgo

Waning Gibbous Moon
Boxing Day Bank Holiday Substitute – UK

---
29 Tuesday
Virgo • VOC (16h 10m)

Waning Gibbous Moon Phase ends

---
30 Wednesday
VOC • Libra

Last Quarter Moon 09°05' Libra

---
31 Thursday
Libra

Waning Crescent Moon Phase starts
New Years Eve

---
1 Friday
Libra • VOC (6h 49m) • Scorpio

Waning Crescent Moon
2027 begins with Jupiter, Uranus and Chiron in Retrograde
New Years Day

January 2027

Journalling and Notes

---

2   **Saturday**

Scorpio

Waning Crescent Moon

---

3   **Sunday**

Scorpio • VOC (7h 25m) • Sagittarius

Waning Crescent Moon

New Year Wishes and Intentions for 2027

Happy Manifesting in 2027!

The Moon in the Zodiac Signs

Moon in Aries.
At this emotionally powerful time, use the energy to be assertive and to initiate your ideas. Say how it is and take action.

Moon in Taurus.
Grounded, sensual, and earthy, use this energy to attune yourself with the natural rhythms of nature. A great time for walking meditations.

Moon in Gemini.
A time of communication, reaching out and connecting with others, use this energy for networking and socializing.

Moon in Cancer.
A wonderful time to be at home, share food, and be in the company of family and close friends. Use this energy to nourish your soul, spending time with those you love.

Moon in Leo.
Sing, laugh, express yourself and find your voice. Use this energy to feel alive and embrace the joy of self-discovery and self-expression. You are never too old to play!

Moon in Virgo.
This energy supports attention to detail bringing focus, dedication, structure, order, and precision. Approach your tasks with willingness and a desire to serve.

Moon in Libra.
The energy of this Moon calls for harmony and balance. This is a time to share and to discover yourself through your relationships and the company of others.

Moon in Scorpio.
A time to journey inwards, this energy connects you to the depths of your unconscious and can bring deep emotions to the surface. Be sure to listen to yourself and take your yearnings seriously.

Moon in Sagittarius.
The energy of this Moon invites you to vision in an optimistic future, full of hope and possibility. A great time to expand your horizons and dream big!

Moon in Capricorn.
The energy of this Moon invites you to take pragmatic, practical actions to manifest your ideas into form. Get building and embrace the joy of doing.

Moon in Aquarius.
A time to collaborate, share ideas, and work together. The energy of this Moon invites you to align your individual contribution with a higher vision of greater purpose that will also serve the collective Soul of humanity.

Moon in Pisces.
A time to dream and a time to heal. Open yourself to divine inspiration and allow yourself to be guided. The energy of this Moon brings illumination, fuelling imagination and creativity.

VOC - Void of Course Moon

The Moon is the Earths satellite, and as she travels around our beautiful planet, from our perspective and viewpoint here on Earth, she passes through each of the 12 signs of the Zodiac… and as this happens, the Lunar energy is channeled through the energetic resonance or personality of that sign. Whilst passing through each of the Zodiac signs, she also connects with and collaborates with any of the other planetary influences that are currently connected with that particular sign.

The Moon both influences these planetary happenings… sometimes adding weight to them and sometimes softening them, depending on the Moon phase… and in turn, these planetary alliances also flavour the essence and energy of the incoming Lunar influence.

When the Moon is noted as 'Void of Course', (VOC) it means that the Moon is no longer connected to any planetary collaborations that are currently resonant with a sign and so the Lunar energy is free from additional planetary influences. The 'Void of Course' period ends when the Moon enters the next Zodiac sign… and this period can last for minutes… or sometimes several hours… and I have noticed that this 'Void of Course' space affects people in uniquely individual ways…

For some, this Lunar freedom can feel quite liberating, creating a natural channel for insights, illuminations, and even increased motivation to flow through… however, for others, particularly during periods of extreme change and transition, the void of course Moon can feel a bit unanchored and directionless.

I have personally found it extremely helpful to notice how the void of course space affects me and to be aware ahead of time of any particularly long void of course periods… especially when my world is particularly busy!

For up-to-date Void of Course Moon information you can follow Jenny's Moon updates on YouTube

- https://www.youtube.com/c/MoonMagicWeeklyTarot

Solar and Lunar Eclipses

During eclipse season, the already intense energy of both the New and Full Moons is intensified. An eclipse in your sign will always be a significant trigger point or turning point in your own personal process of evolution and can often herald random events that create sudden and unexpected changes.

Symbolized in the tarot pack by the cards of Death and the Tower, the energy of both the solar and lunar eclipses are associated with transformation, either internally or in the circumstances of your external world and often herald both endings and new beginnings.

Eclipses are also associated with your Karmic journey… it is said that during eclipse season an energetic portal is opened that enables you to see beyond your usual perception of time… with opportunity to connect your past, your present, and your future, and discover your purpose and calling in this present moment.

On your personal journey of manifestation, understanding this heightened and intensified energy is incredibly helpful… you can plan when to reflect… when to set your intentions… and when to take action to move something forwards… particularly when you want to make or initiate significant changes in any aspect of your life.

I have personally found that the best way to work with the influence of the eclipses, is to consciously make time to slow down… and let the Universe show the way. So rather than trying to control events… get still… and practice the art of allowing… and be responsive to whatever shows up rather than trying to take the lead… and then take action accordingly.

Solar Eclipse.

A solar eclipse is when the Moon sits in between the Sun and the Earth, with the Moon covering the Sun. This will always occur at a New Moon. The energy associated with this time is the same as a New Moon, but intensified, like a New Moon on steroids!

This is the perfect time to get still and to meditate into a space of personal dreamtime and allow your ideas to flow.

The energy of a solar eclipse can bring an extraordinary surge of creative possibilities, although these may not always arrive in the shape or form that you expect... so if you're already involved in setting wishes and intentions, but then find that something happens to suddenly create a shift in your direction, trust that this unexpected change is important to your personal growth and evolution and connected to the calling of your soul. In matters of manifestation, the universe will always have the upper hand and tends to bring us what we need... although not always what we want!

When you can trust that even in moments of upheaval and disruption you are being gifted with an opportunity, you open yourself to receive the fullest potential and the greatest learning to be found in every situation.

Lunar Eclipse.

A lunar eclipse is when the earth sits between the Moon and the Sun, and this will always occur at a Full Moon. Full Moons are associated with heightened emotions and during a lunar eclipse, emotions can run high, like a Full Moon on steroids!

At the time of a lunar eclipse, the energy of the Moon is like a fully charged battery, highly charged and ready to ignite change.

In the illumination of the Full Moon at her most powerful, all is revealed.

Anything and everything that is running smoothly and working in service of a balanced and authentic life will be apparent to you, confirming that you are walking the right path... likewise, anything and everything that is not working for you or no longer serving you, both internally and externally, will also be brought into the light, calling to be addressed, changed, and if necessary, changed... let go of... and released.

As long as something remains hidden or unconscious, you are helpless to address the issue and to take actions of resolution, but when you identify a problem, the very fact that you can see the issue clearly creates an opportunity to seek solutions and find ways forward.

On your personal journey of manifestation, the energy of a lunar eclipse increases your connections with any emotional residue from the past that may be clinging and coloring your perspectives inappropriately... this creates an amazing opportunity for cleansing and release, clearing the way for resolution and healing. This is a powerful time to embrace forgiveness... of both yourself... and others.

If you are struggling with any difficult emotions this book will help you to understand your Emotions as a source of empowerment... yes... even the tough ones!

- Mindfulness meets Emotional Awareness - 7 Steps to Learn the Language of your Emotions - https://www.amazon.com/author/jennyflorence

Lunar eclipses are also often associated with external changes that are a mirror or a reflection of your internal growth and learning... so whatever is taking place around you, if something in your life appears to be needing to change or to leave, let go gracefully and know that it is timely for the evolution of your soul.

If you are naturally a highly empathic person and particularly sensitive to the feelings of others, at the time of a lunar eclipse you may find yourself highly absorbent to the emotional states of the people around you... so be sure to cleanse and do a daily release ceremony to let go of anything that doesn't belong to you, before meditating into your own space of illumination.

- 17th February – New Moon *Annular Solar Eclipse 28°56' Aquarius
- 3rd March –- Full Moon Total Lunar Eclipse 12°51' Virgo
- 12th August – New Moon Total Solar Eclipse 20°08' Leo
- 28th August – Full Moon Partial Lunar Eclipse 04°51' Pisces

* An Annular Solar Eclipse happens when the Moon's orbit takes her farther away from Earth... and so from our visual perspective when she passes directly between the Sun and Earth, she appears smaller than the Sun... and this creates a bright ring around the Moon... and this is known as a Ring of Fire.

The Planets in Retrograde

The Inner Planets, Mercury, Venus, and Mars.

Mercury in Retrograde.

- 26th February 22° 33' Pisces – 20th March 08° 29' Pisces
- 29th June 26° 15' Cancer – 23rd July 16° 18' Cancer
- 24th October 20° 58' Scorpio – 13th November 05° 02' Scorpio

Mercury retrograde periods are associated with disruption, obstructions, and delays… plans go astray, and we often experience roadblocks and diversions, and difficulties with IT and communication systems… so in our target and goal orientated culture, this tends to be viewed through a very negative lens…

However, if you step away from this viewpoint and consider that all aspects of planetary influences are bringing valuable and necessary gifts, this shift in perspective means you can stand back and work with the incoming energy. This is not the time to plough forwards and to push and to strive… this will come soon enough, and if you use the retrograde period well you will be wiser and better placed to move ahead with ease.

At a level of Soul growth and natural evolution, the influence of Mercury invites you to develop wisdom… so when this planet appears to travel backwards, the energy is calling you to slow down, take your time, and be alert to any signals and signs that the universe is trying to bring you… so if something is getting in the way, or a diversion pops up seemingly out of nowhere, the universe may be giving you an important sign… perhaps you are meant to take an alternative route where you will discover something that was absolutely essential to your personal growth and evolution.

Past issues can also show up during a Mercury retrograde period, so if something from your past raises its head then your attention is required. This is an invitation for you to acknowledge this and take the time to do whatever is needed to sort it out and if needed, lay it to rest.

Venus in Retrograde.

- 3rd October 08° 29' Scorpio – 14th November 22° 51' Libra

Are you in balance? Do you allow yourself to receive as much as you give and vice versa... are you actively involved in your own self-care... do you pause to celebrate your achievements along the way... and do you give yourself an appropriate amount of time out to relax?

Self-care is not an act of selfishness... it is an act of consciousness. When Venus moves into retrograde the energy of the feminine invites you to listen to your heart... to override the demands of a busy mind... and be centred in your truest values... including and especially your own self-care.

Venus in retrograde is a wonderful time to reflect and to realign and to rebalance in all areas of your life. This revitalizing influence will keep your energy clean and flowing and ensure that your energetic resonance is congruent with all that you wish to manifest into the world. As such, Venus in retrograde plays an essential role in your ability to manifest your truest desires.

During periods of transition, if you have ever found yourself questioning what your true calling might be, when Venus is in retrograde, ask for guidance and be open to receive.

If during this time you find yourself called to stand up for your values, the female warrior energy of Venus will support you in connecting with the lioness within. In the name of kindness, compassion and peace, her retrograde energy will encourage you to find your authentic voice, speak your truth, and stand firm in your boundaries.

Mars in Retrograde.

- **There is no Mars Retrograde in 2026**

When Mars moves into a retrograde motion you are invited to reassess your progress, not only the projects, relationships, and circumstances of your external world, but also the way that you set about acquiring and achieving these goals.

Mars in retrograde will often highlight the role that certain emotions play in the process of manifestation, for example, anger when channeled positively through mindful considered actions, creates assertiveness... however, its negative counterpart can result in aggression and frustration being directed inappropriately, towards both yourself and others... so during this time, be prepared to journey inwards and reassess, not only your needs and desires... but also how you get these met... working from the inside out.

The Transpersonal Planets, Jupiter, and Saturn.

Jupiter in Retrograde.

- 11th November 2025 25° 09' Cancer – 11th March 2026 15° 05' Cancer
- 13th December 2026 27° 01' Leo – 13th April 2027 16° 59' Leo

This is a time of powerful personal growth! Jupiter in retrograde invites you on an inward quest of self-discovery, seeking knowledge and illumination so you can stand in your own truth and walk your talk.

Jupiter is known as the planet of good luck and good fortune and from the perspective of manifestation, the retrograde period can bring experiences that invite you to look within and seek answers of a Spiritual nature, helping you to forge your true values and attune with your greater purpose. And so, during this period windows of opportunity may open that illuminate issues from your past, including past lives, giving you the opportunity to find resolution and align with your true calling at this present moment of your journey.

Any internal growth and changes made during this time will then in turn manifest outwardly when Jupiter returns to a forward flow of expansion. Seriously amazing stuff!

Saturn in Retrograde.

- 26th July 14° 45' Aries – 10th December 07°55' Aries

Saturn is known as Father Time and the planet of Karma and when his energy moves into retrograde, aspects of your life that need restructuring and reorganizing often come to a head, bringing circumstances that show you exactly what is working for you... as well as anything that is not!

For us as humans, the lessons of Saturn can sometimes feel quite harsh, as the energy calls us to account, speaking in the name of 'Tough Love'... however, this is not without major rewards! The more open you are to embracing the natural evolutionary process of 'weeding and pruning'... letting go gracefully of anything that no longer serves or has outlived its purpose... whether these are physical aspects of your life, or internal attitudes and beliefs... then the more smoothly these periods of profound transition will emerge.

Saturn retrograde energy is a reminder that change is both necessary and natural and that we live in a continual space of learning, not only from all the amazing experiences that fill us with joy, but also from the experiences that don't feel so good as well!

From the perspective of manifestation, when you recognize that all your experiences, both good and bad, are a source of inspiration and guidance, then rather than dwell on the negative, you can use every experience to define your desires with greater clarity. This in turn opens you to receive the guidance and direction that you need to manifest those desires that resonate with you at a core level of Soul.

The Outer Planets, Uranus, Neptune, and Pluto.

The energy of the outer planets is slow moving which means that their influence is deep and penetrating, creating significant growth stages with long term implications. In our individual natal charts, the positioning of these planets will not only have personal implications but will also be an indicator of generational traits.

Uranus in Retrograde.

- 6th September 2025 01° 27' Gemini – 4th February 2026 27° 27' Taurus
- 10th September 2026 05° 41' Gemini – 8th February 2027 01° 40' Gemini

Uranus is known as the Great Awakener and the bringer of sudden events that wake you up and let you know that something needs to change... Uranus energy also holds a direction of higher purpose with higher minded and out of the box solutions... often arriving unexpectedly.

When in retrograde, this sometimes-impulsive energy slows down and invites you to take conscious innovative actions that forge new ways of being and living, all with the purpose of liberating you from limiting perspectives and aligning your manifestations with the greater good.

Neptune in Retrograde.

- 7th July 04° 25' Aries – 12th December 01° 36' Aries

Neptune is the planet of creativity, dreams, and imagination, and as such plays a key role in manifestation.

Being so dreamy, the influence of Neptunian energy opens you to divine guidance and spiritual illumination, however… it can also bring so much dreamy energy that you may find it hard to remain grounded or hold your boundaries. This is valuable to know as Neptunian energy can also sometimes indicate confusion and create a vulnerability to people who operate through delusion and deception.

When in retrograde, the Neptunian energy calls you to get real… and this is FAB!

Neptune in retrograde brings heightened levels of intuition and illumination… it's like a 'Spiritual Reality Check' that helps you to see beyond any false illusions that may have previously been holding you back.

These powerful insights can be used to bring clarity of purpose and intent, releasing limiting beliefs and perspectives that may have previously blocked some of your manifestations.

Pluto in Retrograde.
- 6th May 05°30' Aquarius – 16th October 03° 04' Aquarius

Pluto requests transformation and re-birth and naturally invites personal reflection at its most powerful… this influence will tap into your psychological make-up through a deep dive into your unconscious, revealing any shadows from the past that need to be released… purifying and emerging afresh with greater vitality and potency.

When Pluto is in retrograde this is not a time to hold onto or cling to the past… if some aspect of your world seems to be coming to an end, whether internal or external, such as… any outdated thinking patterns or behaviours… or an inappropriate or limiting belief… or an actual situation, circumstance, person, or people… then let go gracefully and allow yourself to emerge into a space of new beginnings.

Chiron and the Consciousness of Healing.

Chiron in Retrograde.

- 30th July 2025 27° 09' Aries – 2nd January 2026 22° 35' Aries
- 3rd August 2026 00° 52' Taurus – 6th January 2027 26° 15' Aries

Chiron embodies the classic architype of the wounded healer. In mythology he is depicted as half man and half beast, able to bring wisdom and to teach and heal others… and yet he cannot heal himself. As an outer influence, his energy is slow moving, signifying profound generational changes.

Astrologically, Chiron is classified as both a planet and a comet, whose journey here is transient. In spiritual circles it is said that his presence will create a rainbow bridge of healing that will lead humanity to a higher plane of consciousness and living… in equality with one another… and in unity with all of life. Many Tribal cultures have legends that speak of all of the life on this planet arriving on the tail of a comet, acknowledging that from a spiritual perspective, we all come from the same source and are all related.

The retrograde energy of Chiron invites you to enter a space of deep cleansing and repair, laying the past to rest and stepping into a space of unity and higher vision.

This level of healing has the potential for us as individuals and as a collective humanity to resolve long-standing historical wounds that have spanned generations, bringing a new and different future for our planet and for generations yet to come.

The Art of Manifestation Oracle Cards

The Art of Manifestation Oracle Cards featured in this diary are available to buy.

Join Jenny's email list via her online Library to receive updates about cards, books, and next year's diary.

https://www.azemotionalhealth.com/

About the Author

Jenny Florence is a best-selling Author. Her career as a professional Accredited BACP, UKRC Registered Counsellor spanned over 28 years working with individuals, couples, and teams.

She is the founder and creator of the A-Z of Emotional Health on-line Video Library, a free online Resource, dedicated to understanding Emotional and Mental Wellness from a holistic perspective.

She has been reading Tarot Cards and Runes since she was a teenager and has also studied astrology.

Her books and cards include:

- 7 Steps to Spiritual Empathy – Learn to Listen, Change your Life!
- Mindfulness meets Emotional Awareness - 7 Steps to Learn the Language of your Emotions
- I Choose Love – the A-Z Guidebook for the Spiritual Warrior
- Manifest with the Moon Astro-Moon Diary
- The Art of Manifestation Oracle Cards

For extra Moon Information, Readings & Webinars, Books, Cards, and Courses, follow Jenny on social media or visit her websites

- https://www.youtube.com/c/MoonMagicWeeklyTarot
- https://www.youtube.com/c/MoonMagicMonthlyTarot
- https://www.instagram.com/moonmagicjennyflorence/
- https://moonmagicmastertarot.com/
- https://www.azemotionalhealth.com/

To access extra video material and support Jenny's free online library join her Patreon community.

- https://www.patreon.com/AZEmotionalHealth

www.ingramcontent.com/pod-product-compliance
Lightning Source LLC
Chambersburg PA
CBHW032223080426
42735CB00008B/696